i

ii

DAVIES

FIFTH BUSINESS

NOTES

COLES EDITORIAL BOARD

'Bound to stay open

Publisher's Note

Otabind (Ota-bind). This book has been bound using the patented Otabind process. You can open this book at any page, gently run your finger down the spine, and the pages will lie flat.

ABOUT COLES NOTES

COLES NOTES have been an indispensible aid to students on five continents since 1948.

COLES NOTES are available for a wide range of individual literary works. Clear, concise explanations and insights are provided along with interesting interpretations and evaluations.

Proper use of COLES NOTES will allow the student to pay greater attention to lectures and spend less time taking notes. This will result in a broader understanding of the work being studied and will free the student for increased participation in discussions.

COLES NOTES are an invaluable aid for review and exam preparation as well as an invitation to explore different interpretive paths.

COLES NOTES are written by experts in their fields. It should be noted that any literary judgement expressed herein is just that – the judgement of one school of thought. Interpretations that diverge from, or totally disagree with any criticism may be equally valid.

COLES NOTES are designed to supplement the text and are not intended as a substitute for reading the text itself. Use of the NOTES will serve not only to clarify the work being studied, but should enhance the readers enjoyment of the topic.

ISBN 0-7740-3296-0

© COPYRIGHT 1997 AND PUBLISHED BY
COLES PUBLISHING COMPANY
TORONTO - CANADA
PRINTED IN CANADA

Manufactured by Webcom Limited
Cover finish: Webcom's Exclusive **DURACOAT**

iv

CONTENTS

About the Author

Elspeth Cameron grew up in Barrie, Ontario and studied at the University of British Columbia and University of New Brunswick. She obtained her Ph.D. at McGill in Montreal. She is the author of two books: *Robertson Davies* and *Hugh MacLennan: A Writer's Life*. She has written many articles on Canadian literature and a number of reviews for *Saturday Night*.

Robertson Davies: Life and Works

Robertson Davies was born on August 28, 1913, in the small Ontario town of Thamesville. To others, his parents "both made an instantaneous impression of quite extraordinary force — forces that must either make or break a sensitive child." Senator Rupert William Davies and his wife, Florence, introduced their third son, Robertson, to a love of drama at an early age. At three he made his first stage appearance as an Israelite child in the biblical opera *Queen Esther*. Davies' father was owner and editor of the Thamesville *Herald*, and his financial success with this local newspaper enabled him to send his son to Upper Canada College in Toronto for an expensive education.

As a young man, Davies pursued his education in arts at Queen's University in Kingston where he had to be given special permission to enrol because he had failed to pass the entrance requirements in mathematics. Davies went on to obtain a B. Litt. degree in 1938 from Balliol College at Oxford University in England. His thesis was called *Shakespeare's Boy Actors*, and it was published the following year.

At this time, Davies had ambitions to become an actor himself. While a student, he took small parts in companies that toured the English countryside and, when he finished his degree, he joined the famous Old Vic Repertory Theatre. There he was given a number of minor roles — usually those of the buffoon or eccentric. He played Romeo's father in Shakespeare's *Romeo and Juliet*, for example. He also did some literary work for the director, tried his hand at directing, pitched in with stage managing and taught in the school associated with the theater. In 1940, he married an Australian girl named Brenda Mathews whom he had met at Oxford and who had also come to work at the Old Vic.

Late in 1940, wartime conditions forced Davies to give up his acting ambitions and he returned with his new wife to Canada to take up the position of literary editor of *Saturday Night*. After two years in this job, he moved to Peterborough where he became editor of the Peterborough *Examiner*.

For the next fifteen years as editor, and for ten years after that as publisher of this newspaper, he worked hard all day at his office and turned to his own writing in the evening. During those years he managed to publish 18 books, produce several plays and write many articles for other newspapers and journals. In addition, for the three years when Ontario's Stratford Festival came into existence, from 1953-55, he invested a great deal of time and energy collaborating with Tyrone Guthrie and Grant Macdonald to launch it successfully. Part of this collaboration involved the publishing of a book on each season's plays: *Renown at Stratford* (1953), *Twice Have the Trumpets Sounded* (1954) and *Thrice the Brinded Cat Hath Mew'd* (1955).

While editor of the Peterborough *Examiner*, Davies wrote a syndicated column called "The Diary of Samuel Marchbanks" in which he lampooned local customs and attitudes. These columns he later collected into his three "Marchbanks" books: *The Diary of Samuel Marchbanks* (1947), *The Table-Talk of Samuel Marchbanks* (1949) and *Marchbanks' Almanack* (1967).

As far as his plays were concerned, Davies was not a prophet unrecognized in his own land. His play, *Eros at Breakfast* (1948), won the Dominion Drama Festival award for the best one-act play. His next play, *Fortune, My Foe* (1949), won the Dominion Drama award for the best Canadian play that year. At the same competition, Davies also won an award for his direction of Shakespeare's *The Taming of the Shrew*. The following year, he wrote *At My Heart's Core*, a drama based on the pioneer life of Susanna Moodie and her sister Catherine Parr Traill. His best play to date is one of his earliest, *Overlaid* (1948), a satiric study of cultural deprivation in the rural outposts of Canada.

In 1951, Davies added fiction, the genre in which he would excel, to his journalism and drama. *Tempest-tost* is set in the small town of Salterton which is based on Kingston, Ontario where he had attended Queen's University. The plot concerns the hilarious happenings that surround a production of *The Tempest* by a little theater group which does not have the sophistication necessary to bring Shakespeare to the stage. This was to be the first of three novels that would come to be called "The Salterton Trilogy." The second, *Leaven of Malice* (1954), concerned the uproarious events that followed on a practical joke in Salterton. This book won the Stephen Leacock Medal for Humour. *A Mixture of Frailties* (1958), the third book in this trilogy, though still satirical, struck a more serious note. Here Davies showed that a talented singer from Salterton would have to go abroad, away from the unripened cultural environment of Canada, if her abilities were to be developed properly.

The success of *Leaven of Malice* led Davies to attempt to write a play based on it called *Love and Libel*, but the play failed dismally in New York, mainly because it was a collaborative effort. This did not discourage Davies from continuing to write and produce plays, however. Of special note are the two masques he wrote to be performed by the boys of Upper Canada College: *A Masque of Aesop* (1952) and *A Masque of Mr. Punch* (1963). His most recent plays are *Question Time* (1975) and *Pontiac and the Green Man* (1980) in the last of which Davies and his wife played leading roles.

In the 1960s, Davies began to reap the rewards of his energetic life. In 1960, the same year that he published a collection of his serious thoughts on literature called *A Voice From the Attic*, he was awarded the Lorne Pierce Medal for distinguished service to Canadian literature. That same year, he joined the staff at the University of Toronto where he taught courses in drama. In 1963, he was also appointed Master of Massey College, the University's new graduate college, where he would remain until his retirement at the age of 68 in 1981. In 1967, he was invited to become a Fellow of the Royal Society of Canada and soon he began receiving honourary degrees from a series of Canadian universities.

It might have seemed to others that Davies had reached the summit of his writing career that decade, but he surprised everyone, for it was the novel *Fifth Business* (1970), which proved to be his best work and firmly established Davies as a major literary figure. The serious note which had been sounded beneath the satirical surface of *A Mixture of Frailties*, the novel that preceded it, had developed into a full concern for man's spiritual salvation. Although the novel is by no means devoid of humour, it raises questions of great importance for all human beings. The tremendous success of this novel, which was not set in Salterton but in the fictional town of Deptford, based on Davies' home town of Thamesville, led him to consider a second and then a third novel related to the first. Thus, *The Manticore* (1972) and *World of Wonders* (1975) came to be considered "The Deptford Trilogy," although Davies never set out to write a series.

Nor was Davies content to conclude his writing career with

World of Wonders. His latest novel, *The Rebel Angels* (1981), is a rollicking tale of the goings-on at a college known as "Spook," roughly based on Trinity College at the University of Toronto, and "Ploughwright College," based on Massey College. With the freedom from teaching and administrative duties that retirement affords, Davies promises to keep on producing excellent work, for he has said that it is the years over 70 that are the most productive.

Works

Essays

Shakespeare's Boy Actors	1939
The Diary of Samuel Marchbanks	1947
The Table-Talk of Samuel Marchbanks	1949
Renown at Stratford	1953
Twice Have the Trumpets Sounded	1954
Thrice the Brinded Cat Hath Mew'd	1955
A Voice From the Attic	1960
Shakespeare for Young Players	1964
Marchbanks' Almanack	1967
One Half of Robertson Davies	1977
The Enthusiasms of Robertson Davies	1979
The Well-Tempered Critic	1981

Novels

Tempest-Tost	1951
Leaven of Malice	1954
A Mixture of Frailties	1958
Fifth Business	1970
The Manticore	1972
World of Wonders	1975
The Rebel Angels	1981

Plays

Overlaid	1948
Eros at Breakfast and Other Plays	1949
Fortune, My Foe	1949
At My Heart's Core	1950
A Masque of Aesop	1952
A Jig for the Gypsy	1954

A Masque of Mr. Punch 1963
Hunting Stuart and Other Plays 1972
Question Time 1975
Pontiac and the Green Man 1980

Introduction to *Fifth Business*

Davies once claimed that in writing *Fifth Business* he was "trying to record the bizarre and passionate life of the Canadian people." For many years, writers like Morley Callaghan, Hugh MacLennan, Margaret Laurence and Mordecai Richler had been attempting in various ways to define the Canadian identity in their works. With *Fifth Business*, Davies dramatized his version of his nation's character. In showing the "bizarre and passionate" life of Dunstan Ramsay that lay concealed beneath his apparent personality — that of a doddering old schoolmaster — Davies showed that while Canadians may *appear* to be quiet and dull, they have an inner life which is exciting. He intended this idea to apply to Canada generally: while Canada is not a top power among nations, it has played the role of Fifth Business on the world stage.

Fifth Business gains much of its force and vitality from the fact that the circumstances Davies portrays closely resemble his own experience. Deptford is similar to Thamesville where Davies grew up; Colborne College resembles Upper Canada College where Davies went to school; Ramsay's career as a scholar and as a teacher of unusual kinds of knowledge parallels Davies'. This is not to say, however, that the novel is autobiographical. On the contrary, Davies simply uses his own experiences as a springboard from which to give his imagination a point of departure. However, the novel's unity of tone probably arises from the degree to which its central character, Dunstan Ramsay, is a man close in temperament to his author.

Above all, Ramsay is like Davies in valuing the spiritual far more than the physical or material. Davies, like Ramsay, is a religious man, not so much in the conventional sense of going to church, but in the wider sense. Both men acknowledge and revere powers beyond the human which play a strong role in man's destiny. Because Davies demonstrates and supports this view of life, he can be seen to belong to the long tradition of Christian humanism which has characterized Canadian thought and culture.

After the outstanding success of *Fifth Business*, enjoyed well beyond Canada's borders when it was published, Davies decided to write two further novels related to it. These three novels came to be known as "The Deptford Trilogy." *The Manticore* (1972) centers on the nervous breakdown of Boy

Staunton's son, David, after his father's death. Developing the theories of Jungian psychology which he had subtly employed in *Fifth Business*, Davies based this novel on the psychoanalysis of David. In *World of Wonders* (1975), Davies turns to an exploration of the life story of Magnus Eisengrim as told from his own point of view.

Of the three novels that form "The Deptford Trilogy" and, indeed of all his novels and other works, *Fifth Business* remains Davies' best-known and most successful creative work.

Characters in the Novel

Athelstan, Cece: A foul-mouthed, alcoholic bum in Deptford. He is the black sheep of the Athelstan family, the oldest family in town.

Blazon, Padre Ignacio: An eccentric Jesuit Bollandist whom Ramsay meets in Brussels and who travels with him on the train to Vienna. He encourages Ramsay to find out who Mary Dempster is in his "personal mythology."

Bowyer, Reverend Andrew: The Presbyterian minister in Deptford at the time Dunstable Ramsay is a boy.

Cruikshank, Ben: A carpenter in Deptford and father of Leola. He does not want her to marry Boy Staunton.

Cruikshank, Leola: The village beauty who marries Boy Staunton. She is the first girl Ramsay falls in love with, mainly because she is so pretty.

Delehaye, Père Hippolyte: A Jesuit and editor of the *Acta Sanctorum*. He encourages Ramsay to publish his work about the saints.

Dempster, Reverend Amasa: The Baptist minister in Deptford who resigns his job because of his wife's disgrace. Later he works in the sawmill.

Dempster, Mary: Married to the Reverend Amasa Dempster, she is a simple but religious woman whose adultery disgraces her husband. This action results in one of the three "miracles" which makes her Ramsay's "fool-saint."

Dempster, Paul: Their son, born prematurely, who runs away at age nine to join a circus. He becomes a magician under the name of Faustus Legrand and, later, Magnus Eisengrim.

Edward VIII: Heir to the throne of England and later King until his abdication. He is an acquaintance of Boy Staunton's.

Eisengrim, Magnus: A magician whom Ramsay encounters in Guadalupe and recognizes as Paul Dempster from Deptford.

Faustina: A beautiful girl in Eisengrim's magic show with whom Ramsay falls briefly in love.

Headmaster (of Colborne College): The person to whom Ramsay addresses his letter of protest about the way he has been portrayed at his retirement from teaching at the College.

Heighington, Mabel: A Deptford girl with a loose reputation who is caught in a sexual embrace with Boy Staunton.

Hornick, Denyse: An intelligent, determined woman, she is a strong supporter of women's rights. She becomes Boy's second wife after Leola's death.

Hornick, Lorene: She is Denyse's daughter from her first marriage. She is 13 years old, heavy, short and clumsy, and is enrolled in a special school for slow learners.

King George V: King of England and father of Edward VIII. He presents Ramsay with his Victoria Cross at Buckingham Palace in London.

Leadbeater, Reverend George Maldon: A well-paid minister from a fashionable church in New York who impresses Boy Staunton on board ship with his materialistic interpretation of Christianity.

Marfleet, Canon: Diana's father and an Anglican priest who ministers to the Royal Family at Windsor Castle. He also has his own parish in Buckinghamshire, England.

Marfleet, Diana: The English nurse who takes care of Ramsay while he is in a coma following severe wounds in the war. She is Ramsay's first lover and he almost marries her.

Marfleet, Mrs.: Diana's mother and a member of the English aristocracy. She is a pretty, strong-willed woman who pretends to be brainless.

McCausland, Dr.: The Ramsays' doctor in Deptford, a staunch Presbyterian with a "no-nonsense" attitude to life.

Packer, Lorne: The graduate student whose condescending write-up of Dunstan Ramsay's retirement in the *College Chronicle* prompts Ramsay to write the story of his life.

Papple, Milo: A boy Ramsay went to school with who is an expert at rude, practical jokes. He later replaces his father as town barber.

Papple, Myron: Milo's father and the town barber, given to gossip and gum-chewing. He plays the Kaiser in the homecoming procession that welcomes Ramsay after the war.

Ramsay, Alexander: Ramsay's father, and editor and owner of the *Deptford Banner*. He is considered a learned and literary man in Deptford.

Ramsay, Dunstable: He is the main character whose life story constitutes the novel. He is also called "Dunny" as a young boy and later "Dunstan" when renamed by Diana.

Ramsay, Mrs.: Ramsay's mother, a determined and powerful woman of considerable influence in Deptford.

Ramsay, William: Dunstan's brother who is also called Willie. He works at his father's office, falls ill and "dies" after an accident at work. He is killed in World War I as a soldier in France.

Shanklin, Miss Bertha: Mrs. Dempster's aunt, who takes her to live in Weston after Amasa has died and Paul has run away.

Staunton, Caroline: Daughter of Boy and Leola. She is a spoiled girl given to tantrums.

Staunton, Dr.: Also known as "Doc", he is Boy's father. He spends more time acquiring property with tobacco and sugar beet crops than he does being a doctor.

Staunton, Edward David: Boy and Leola's son and a boarder at Colborne College from age ten to 18. He is named after Edward VIII.

Staunton, Percy Boyd: Ramsay's "friend" from Deptford who marries Leola Cruikshank. He becomes a successful businessman and makes a lot of money, but he is not entirely happy. He is to be contrasted with Ramsay.

Surgeoner, Joel: The tramp who makes love to Mrs. Dempster in the gravel pit and later converts to become a minister as a result. He is eventually head of the Lifeline Mission in Toronto.

Vitzlipützli, Liselotte: Also known as "Liesl", she is a huge, ugly, Swiss woman whose money finances Eisengrim's magic show. She also is the business manager and mechanic for the show, and eventually becomes good friends with Ramsay.

Wettenhall, Orpheus: Miss Bertha Shanklin's lawyer. He shoots himself when she dies because he has embezzled her money and the money of others.

Plot Summary

Insulted by an article describing his career as that of a dull, old schoolmaster, Dunstan Ramsay writes his memoirs for his Headmaster. He intends his story, which will be released only after his death, as a justification of his life which will reveal that it has been fascinating and useful. The role he has played has been that of Fifth Business.

Ramsay begins with an event in his small home town of Deptford that has shaped his whole life. His pregnant neighbour, Mary Dempster, is accidentally hit on the head when the ten-year-old Ramsay dodges a snowball thrown by his friend Percy Boyd Staunton. The premature birth of her son, Paul, and her own decline into simple-mindedness cause Ramsay to feel profoundly guilty. He becomes fascinated with Mrs. Dempster and sees her as a special person with heroic or saintly qualities, even after she is ostracised by the townspeople for committing adultery with a tramp. When his brother is dying, she seems to Ramsay to be a miracle-worker, for she apparently brings him back from the dead. Ramsay also befriends her son, Paul, and teaches him to do magic tricks.

Eventually, Ramsay rebels against the narrowness of Deptford life and the tyranny of his domineering mother and goes off to fight in the First World War. In the army, he is a loner who seems odd to his fellow-soldiers because he spends his time reading the New Testament. In the famous battle at Passchendaele in France, Ramsay stumbles into a German machine gun nest, kills the three Germans and is later awarded the Victoria Cross for bravery. He does not realize that he has received this award, however, until several months later because he has collapsed in pain after being wounded. Just before he loses consciousness he sees a statue of the Madonna which looks like Mary Dempster.

When he emerges from his long coma, he has lost his left leg and finds himself in a private hospital in England being cared for by an attractive nurse called Diana Marfleet. Diana falls in love with him, takes him to meet her cultured parents and almost succeeds in getting him to marry her. But Ramsay finds her too motherly and eludes her. She changes his name from Dunstable to "Dunstan," after St. Dunstan, before they part good friends.

Ramsay returns to Canada after the war and obtains an

M.A. in history. He then joins the staff of Colborne College, a private school for boys in Toronto, where he will teach for the next forty years. He continues his friendship with Percy Boyd Staunton from Deptford who now lives in Toronto and calls himself "Boy." Boy has pursued a different course in life than Ramsay. He has worked ambitiously to develop his father's sugar beet interests around Deptford into an industrial empire that includes many companies related to sugar production. He has married Leola Cruikshank, the village beauty of Deptford, whom Ramsay also wanted to marry. Boy is important enough to be an official accompanying the Prince of Wales on his tour of Canada in 1927.

During the summers, when he is free of teaching duties, Ramsay has taken up a study which fascinates him. He travels to Europe doing research about saints. Eventually, this research results in a series of articles and books on the subject. In the back of his mind, Ramsay wants to have Mrs. Dempster declared a saint.

This interest in saints puts Ramsay in touch with the Bollandists in Brussels, a special branch of the Jesuit order of priests who have dedicated their lives to publishing material about saints. He particularly makes a friend of Padre Ignacio Blazon, whose eccentricity is combined with deep insight into spiritual matters. From him, Ramsay acquires greater wisdom. Blazon tells Ramsay that finding out whether Mrs. Dempster is a saint is not as important as establishing what mythological role she has played in his life.

In Toronto during the winters, Ramsay becomes Boy's confidante, especially in relation to Leola. Boy has tried to help Leola keep pace with his dizzying climb to power and social status, but she is unable to live up to his ambitions. When she discovers that he has sought comfort with mistresses in Montreal — a discovery which occurs at the same time that the Prince of Wales, now Edward VIII, abdicates — she tries to commit suicide. Although she turns to Ramsay that night, he rejects her. Boy continues to neglect Leola and their two children, David and Caroline, until she becomes sick. When she dies of pneumonia in 1942, Boy does not even bother to return from England where he is working as Minister of Food during the Second World War. Instead, he leaves Ramsay to cope with the funeral.

Boy, all this time, has been giving Ramsay financial advice

so that he can invest his money profitably. When the stock market crashes in 1929, for example, Boy warns Ramsay so that he doesn't go bankrupt. The money Ramsay saves through Boy's advice enables him to support Mrs. Dempster in a mental institution for many years after her husband dies and her son, Paul, runs away from home at the age of nine. It also enables him to continue his scholarly work on the saints which involves expensive, annual trips abroad.

On one of these trips, he coincidentally meets Paul Dempster who has become a skilful conjurer in a travelling circus in the Tyrol, but Paul does not want news of Canada or of his mother whom he blames for his unhappy life. Fifteen years later, on a trip to Mexico, Ramsay again encounters Paul who has become an even more skilful magician called Magnus Eisengrim.

Ramsay temporarily joins Eisengrim's troupe to be a consultant and to ghost-write Eisengrim's autobiography, which he does with imagination and style. While staying with the company, he temporarily becomes infatuated with the beautiful assistant, Faustina. He also gets to know the hideous Liesl who forces him to come to terms with some unpleasant truths about himself. He becomes her lover and lifelong friend.

Eventually, Mrs. Dempster becomes seriously ill and dies, leaving Ramsay to come to terms with her supposed saintliness. Boy Staunton remarries, this time to a determined and clever divorcée, called Denyse Hornick, who is involved in the political campaign for women's rights. Although Boy fails as a Conservative politician, Denyse assists him to manoeuvre his way to an appointment as Lieutenant-Governor of Ontario.

At the time of this appointment, Boy dies under mysterious circumstances. Eisengrim has brought his show to Toronto, and he and Ramsay invite Boy to join them for drinks. The three men recall their pasts in Deptford and Ramsay forces Boy to admit that he put a stone in the snowball that hit Mrs. Dempster. Ramsay has kept the egg-shaped stone as a paperweight and shows it to Boy. At the end of the evening, Boy drives Eisengrim to his hotel. Boy is later found with the stone in his mouth in his sealed car at the bottom of the Toronto harbour. When Ramsay later hears an ambiguous statement in Eisengrim's magic show about the group of five who caused the death, he has a heart attack. Eventually he goes to Switzerland to join Eisengrim and Liesl where he recovers and writes his memoirs.

Chapter by Chapter
Summaries and Commentaries

NOTE: All quotations are from *Fifth Business*, Robertson Davies. Penguin Books, 1977.

PART ONE • CHAPTER 1

Summary

It was the 27th of December, 1908, when something happened to the ten-year-old boy, Dunstable Ramsay, that would involve him with his neighbour, Mrs. Mary Dempster, for the rest of his life. He had been out sledding with his friend, Percy Boyd Staunton, and they had quarrelled because Percy's new Christmas sled would not go as fast as Dunny's.

Percy's family was rich, much wealthier than Dunny's. It seemed unfair to Percy that his more expensive sled wasn't as good as Dunstable's old one. In anger, he began insulting Dunny, bragging that his father was better than Dunny's father. Craftily, Dunny pretended that he was so offended that he was leaving. Actually, he knew it was almost dinner time and he had to be home on time.

Percy followed him on the way home, shouting insults and throwing snowballs. Dunny didn't reply, knowing that was the best way to get even. As he turned onto his street, he checked his new Christmas watch and began to hurry, for it was almost 6:00 p.m.

In front of him walked the Reverend Amasa Dempster, arm in arm with his pregnant wife Mary. Since it was not considered decent for pregnant women to appear in public, the Dempsters always took a walk at this time — after dark when people were having supper. Certain that Percy would try to hit him with one final snowball before he turned into his house, Dunny quickly stepped past the Dempsters and in front of them. Thus, the snowball Percy did, in fact, throw, hit Mrs. Dempster on the back of the head. She cried out and fell down. Her husband might have caught her had he not turned immediately to see who had thrown the snowball. He could not determine who had thrown it.

Instead of darting into his house, Dunny could only stand helpless watching Mrs. Dempster crying and her husband trying to console her with loving words. Feeling guilty because he knew the snowball had been meant for him, he helped Mr. Dempster take his weeping wife home on his sled.

Making excuses for being late for dinner, Dunny told his mother what had happened. He changed his story to make himself appear like a Good Samaritan rather than the guilty cause of the event.

After dinner, Mrs. Ramsay decided to go over to the Dempsters to see if she could help. Even Dr. McCausland considered her an expert in pregnancy and childbirth and, besides, she felt tender towards Mrs. Dempster who was only twenty and unsuited to being a preacher's wife.

Dunny and his brother, Willie, and their father read until 8:30 — the boys' bedtime. Once in bed, Dunny did not fall asleep at once. After an hour he heard his mother return, got up and eavesdropped at the stovepipe that came from the living-room into the upstairs hall.

He heard his mother tell his father to get the baby blankets out of the trunk and some cotton wool from the drugstore. Mrs. Dempster was having her baby prematurely.

At 4:00 a.m. Dunstable heard her come in again, sounding grim, as she reported to his father that Paul Dempster, who was later to become famous by another name, was born on the 28th of December.

Commentary

This opening chapter presents convincingly a child's point of view and offers many insights into the character of that child. Dunny Ramsay is a crafty boy who knows how to get even with his friend Percy and understands the best way to slant the truth so that his mother will not be upset at him for being late for dinner. Being intelligent, he has an enormous curiosity about life: he is fascinated with the "scene" he sees between the injured Mrs. Dempster and her husband and he follows eagerly the drama of the premature birth of Paul. Dunny's intense interest in this drama is the result of his guilt. Feeling strongly that he has been responsible for what has happened, he is frightened and anxious. Characteristically, he keeps his feelings to himself.

Because he is a meticulous boy, he notices every detail of the events in which he takes part. He is able, for example, to give the exact time at which the snowball hit Mrs. Dempster, and he notes with careful accuracy the times at which his mother comes back from the Dempsters'. This gives the reader confidence in him as a narrator.

Many words and phrases in this section have the ring of truth because they are what a child might say or think in the circumstances. Dunny says that his father is reading something "that looked hard and had small print," for example. On the other hand, the event is clearly being remembered by Dunny at a much later stage of his life, for he mentions things the boy would not have known at the time. He says, for example, that Paul Dempster later became famous.

Through Dunny's recollection of this event from childhood, we learn something about his immediate family and about the village of Deptford. His family is orderly and religious. Household rules are strict and well-enforced in a way typical of Presbyterian households of that time. As Dunny sees it, it is his mother who dominates the family. While his father is a shadowy figure who quietly reads, his mother makes decisions such as going to help Mrs. Dempster. Dr. McCausland has once referred to her as having "her head screwed on straight," a compliment which meant that she could be relied on to remain calm in any crisis. Indeed, like most Presbyterians, she does not display emotion, showing neither the tenderness she feels for Mrs. Dempster nor the fears she has for the premature baby. She is "self-possessed." "Scenes," such as the one Dunny sees between the Dempsters in which strong affection is expressed, are considered "very serious breaches of propriety."

The Dempsters, unlike the Ramsays, are Baptists, and we learn that although there are no hard feelings between different religious groups in Deptford, they keep a polite distance. Only in an emergency would someone from another religious group help out.

Davies arouses strong interest in this opening section by treating vividly a highly dramatic event. By indicating that Dunny's involvement with Mrs. Dempster is to be "lifelong" and that Paul Dempster will become famous in later life, Davies makes the reader curious.

CHAPTER 2

Summary

Dunstan explains why he has begun to write the story of his

connection with Mrs. Dempster. His story is actually a report to the Headmaster of Colborne College, the boys' school where he has taught for 45 years. Ramsay has been deeply upset at the write-up of his retirement which was published in the *College Chronicle* in the summer of 1969. Mainly, he objects to the way he was portrayed in the article as a silly old schoolmaster.

Ramsay quotes the article, called "Farewell to the Cork," so that the Headmaster will see what he means. In it, Ramsay appears as someone who has been Assistant Head and Senior History Master for 22 years before he retired. His school nickname has been "Corky." He has survived a heart attack which followed close upon the death of his friend Percy — now known as "Boy" Staunton — who had gained the D.S.O. and C.B.E. after attending Colborne College as a boy and had also become Chairman of the Board of Governors of the school. According to Lorne Packer, the graduate student who has written the article, Ramsay has taught history "as he sees it" to many boys, some of the more famous of whom were present at his retirement. As a retirement gift, the school gave him a tape recorder in the hope that he would use it to put down his recollections of the school's history. They also gave him a tape of the Headmaster's speech praising him and one of the School Choir singing his favorite hymn "For all the saints, Who from their labours rest."

Ramsay indignantly tells the Headmaster that this article reduces him and his work to insignificance. In defence, he points out that it omits mentioning his V.C. (though this does not bother him much). More importantly, it doesn't mention his ten books even though one has been translated into six languages and has sold three-quarters of a million copies, and another one is having a great influence on the history of myth. Nor does it say that he has been the only Protestant contributor to the journal *Analecta Bollandiana* over the last 36 years. Most of all, Ramsay is angry at the attitude of Lorne Packer who makes him seem as if he had never really experienced life fully. Ramsay accuses Packer of having no understanding of religion. He has not been able to see that because of the events of Ramsay's life and character, he has played the role of Fifth Business. Packer, Ramsay claims, wouldn't even be able to comprehend what Fifth Business is if he saw someone playing that role in his own life.

Ramsay turns now to discuss the difficulties of writing

17

about his own childhood. He hopes that he has accurately described the extraordinary night when Paul Dempster was born and that he can go on to continue the story for the Headmaster without presenting himself as a falsely charming, little boy. After years of teaching, he is well aware of the real nature of boys: they are nothing more than a younger version of grown men, complete with bad, as well as good, qualities. He will try to write truthfully about his own past by beginning with a description of the village where he, Percy and Paul were born.

Commentary

This chapter provides a frame of reference for the entire novel. The story which has already begun with Paul Dempster's premature birth is an *apologia pro vita sua* (an explanation of the meaning of one person's life), in this case, Dunstan Ramsay's. Ramsay is propelled by his anger at the superficial account of his life's work which Lorne Packer has written for the school paper. Packer is a contrast to Ramsay in this respect: whereas Packer has only completed his M.A. and is still a young graduate student with a fondness for the "scientific" study of history, Ramsay is a mature and important scholar who has published widely and successfully in an area of history which is not "scientific." Because Packer is blind to the importance of Ramsay's accomplishments, seeing him as nothing more than an old-fashioned, ineffectual schoolmaster, Ramsay comes to his own defence to tell the story of his life to his former Head-master. In doing so, he insists that he will show the truth that lies beneath the surface of his life.

Since it provides the novel's title, the concept of Fifth Business is important. Ramsay uses this idea to explain the type of life he has led. As the epigraph to the novel defines it, in a quotation from Thomas Overskou's *Den Danske Skueplads*, Fifth Business is:

> Those roles which, being neither those of Hero nor Heroine, Confidante nor Villain, but which were nonetheless essential to bring about the Recognition or the dénouement, were called the Fifth Business in drama and opera companies organized according to the old style; the player who acted these parts was often referred to as Fifth Business.

As Ramsay describes it, this role which he has played in life has been "vital though never glorious." In other words, though he has not played a leading role in life's drama, he has not been a mere nobody either.

In many ways, the older man is similar to the boy he once was. Like the young Dunny, the grown Dunstan is observant. He has noticed the tendency of most writers to glorify their own pasts, for example. He is also meticulous in providing exact details of his scholarly work such as the precise length of time (36 years), that he has been writing for the *Analecta Bollandiana*. Unlike the young Dunny, however, the older man does not hold in his emotions, but gives full expression to his anger at Packer, calling him such things as "that ineffable jackass," a "dullard," a "donkey" and a "religious illiterate."

CHAPTER 3

Summary

The village of Deptford seemed to Ramsay neither like the simple and good rural place described in earlier literature nor like the hypocritical vice-ridden places popular in more recent stories. Instead, it was varied in nature, displaying both bad and good traits.

Deptford was located on the Thames River about 15 miles east of Pittstown, the nearest big town. There were about 500 inhabitants, or 800 if the farms were included. There were five churches: the Anglican, the Presbyterian, the Methodist, the Baptist and the Roman Catholic. The village had one lawyer (also the magistrate), one banker in a private bank, two doctors — Dr. McCausland and Dr. Staunton (Percy's father who was becoming rich through real estate dealings), a rough and dirty dentist and an alcoholic veterinarian. There was a canning factory, a sawmill and a few shops.

The oldest family was the Athelstans who had made money in the lumber industry in the 19th century. They owned Deptford's only three-storey house. One of the Athelstans lived across the street from Dunny, a poor old insane woman who tried, from time to time, to escape from her housekeeper. Dunny always tried to help catch her and calm her, even though she didn't like him, because he was curious about what a mad person might say.

Because Dunny's father was the owner and editor of the

weekly paper the *Deptford Banner*, the Ramsays were considered an important family. This was not because the newspaper made a lot of money (it didn't), but because writing the editorials made Mr. Ramsay a literary (or intellectual) leader in the village. Consequently he was on the village Library Board along with the magistrate.

The Ramsays were among the better class of people in the village and they thought well of themselves. Mostly, this was because they were Scottish. Mr. Ramsay had come from Dumfries as a young man, and Mrs. Ramsay's family had been in Canada for three generations without changing the customs common in Scotland. Because of his family's pride in their heritage, Dunny has believed that the Scots were the best people on earth until he was at least 25 years old. It always seemed normal to him that other people in Deptford, who had come mainly from the south of England, should look up to his family. One of his family's main traits, for example, was extreme cleanliness, and the condition of their outdoor toilet set an example for the whole village.

All in all, people in Deptford were serious and proud of their community, especially in comparison to Bowles Corners, a much smaller village about four miles away.

Commentary

This chapter is notable mainly for its humour. Davies describes Deptford with a kindly sense of its shortcomings. As a grown man looking back, he realizes how foolish it was to think that Scots were "the salt of the earth." His description of the churches in Deptford, characterizing them largely by whether or not they were "solvent," indicates the close connection between worldly economic matters and spiritual life in institutions which were supposed to be exclusively spiritual. He lends a comic air to the escapades of the elderly Athelstan woman by comparing her mad dashes into the road to "a hen having a dirt-bath."

Davies' humour is gentle, however, for he recognizes not only the village's weaknesses but also its strengths. It is a close-knit community in which neighbours help one another.

Dunstan also outlines his method as a writer in this section. He says that he will not "pile up details" to give a picture, but will select carefully the most significant details so that his description will be "brief."

CHAPTER 4

Summary

The first six months of Paul Dempster's life were the best time of Mrs. Ramsay's life, but the worst time of Dunny's. A premature baby had much less chance of surviving in 1908 than now, and the situation gave Mrs. Ramsay the greatest challenge ever. Although she was not a trained midwife, she had good sense, a kind heart and the capacity to enjoy being in charge of anything to do with the mysterious female functions. Without her help, Dr. McCausland could not have saved Paul's life.

Dunny continued to eavesdrop at the stovepipe upstairs, so he heard all the details of Paul's condition. This information, much of it new to Dunny, made him feel guilty and even sick.

He learned that Paul had been about 80 days premature. In shock, Mrs. Dempster had had a series of hysterical crying fits. Dr. McCausland had arrived only a quarter of an hour before the birth because he had been busy elsewhere. The baby was so small and so ugly looking that both the doctor and Mrs. Ramsay were frightened. Mr. Dempster fought with the doctor about christening his child. Being a Baptist, he wanted to dip the baby in water, but Dr. McCausland, being a Presbyterian and also concerned not to give the delicate baby a chill, would not let him, and he had to be satisfied with a small sprinkling of water.

Mrs. Ramsay was fascinated with the strange ugliness of the infant. He was red and wrinkled like an old man: his head, back and much of his face were covered with thin, long, black hair. His limbs were tiny and he had almost no nails. His cry sounded like a sick kitten. Even at ten weeks he only weighed three pounds.

They made a nest of jeweller's cotton and hot water bottles with a tent over it into which steam from a kettle was carefully directed. They fed him diluted sweetened milk through a glass fountain-pen filler and some cotton wool. Paul, however, threw most of it up. Mrs. Ramsay decided that he was trying hard to live, so she became determined to fight along with him.

Mr. Dempster was looking after his wife as best he could. Being a Baptist and, therefore, very emotional, he knelt and prayed loudly by her bed until Dr. McCausland told him to stop it as it might upset her further. It seemed to all of them that she was fighting for her life, something Ramsay, looking back, now doubts. In those days, though, childbirth was considered dangerous and more so when there were complications such as these.

Mrs. Ramsay's determined involvement with saving Paul's life meant that she neglected her own family. Mr. Ramsay was proud of his wife's dedication and ability, but Dunny resented the poor meals and lack of attention at home. Paul eventually did gain strength and began to look like a normal baby.

Dunny suffered terribly at this time for several reasons. He still thought he was responsible for the whole dreadful business, and he felt enormous guilt for having dodged the snowball in the first place. When he next saw Percy, he tried to talk about what had happened, but Percy refused to admit that his snowball had hit anyone other than Dunny. Alone with his guilt, Dunny became convinced that he would be damned and go to hell. To complicate matters, it was just during this time that, as an 11-year-old, he entered adolescence. This meant that he was preoccupied with sex, talking secretly about it with other boys at school and suspicious of his parents' intimate life together. To feel that he was responsible for the birth of a child — which now seemed like a grossly sexual act — added to his guilt and disgust. He worried that if he were found out, his mother would reject him.

As if this were not enough, he learned in the spring that, although Paul was going to be all right, Mrs. Dempster seemed unable to recover. She would always be simple-minded as a result of the blow on her head. He felt guilty for that as well.

Commentary

Davies conveys well the guilt and secrecy over sex which are typical of adolescence. In Dunny's case, like that of Stephen Dedalus in James Joyce's *Portrait of the Artist as a Young Man*, his guilt and imagined punishments take shape from the religious tradition in which he has been raised. A characteristic attitude of Presbyterians is implied in his mother's remark that, whoever it was who threw the snowball that caused all this, "the Devil guided his hand." Dunny imagines that he is "of the damned" and that he will suffer the torments of hell in a way similar to the lurid pictures of Gustave Doré which illustrate the family edition of Dante's *Inferno*. The pleasure he feels at his own blossoming sexuality seems sinful to him, since he has been raised to mistrust any sort of pleasure. In a vivid phrase, Davies describes Dunny's state of mind as "the hot craziness of my thinking."

What might be normal feelings in adolescence are intensified by the special events which simply happen to coincide with physical and emotional changes in the 11-year-old boy. Intimate physical details of the birth of Paul which Dunny overhears by eavesdropping actually constitute his sexual education, and he is sometimes sickened by what he learns. His guilt is deepened to the point of serious disturbance — he can't eat or sleep — because of his conviction that he has been responsible for the gross and bizarre birth of Paul.

Davies also provides a clearer picture of Dunny's mother. She is a fiercely determined woman with a "lionlike spirit" who likes to control by doing good for others, in this case for Mrs. Dempster. Ironically, Mrs. Ramsay could do most good at home caring for her own family, especially Dunny who needs reassurance from her at this time. His resentment of her turning her attention from home to the Dempsters is obvious, particularly when he admits that his greatest fear is that his guilt will be punished by rejection by her. But Mrs. Ramsay, with her common sense, does not like any display of emotion. When Mr. Dempster becomes too emotional, she is pleased to hear Dr. McCausland "reading the Riot Act" (as she would put it) to make him stop.

CHAPTER 5

Summary

Though Dunny continued to feel guilty, Mrs. Dempster's simplicity did not seem to be as bad as he had feared. As Mrs. Ramsay said, Mrs. Dempster wasn't really different after the accident; she had always been a bit simple and generally unsuited to being a preacher's wife.

To Dunny, Mrs. Dempster was unusually gentle-looking. She was small, slight and girlish with a soft voice and a happy nature. Her husband was infatuated with her, helping her with the practical tasks of housekeeping that the village people thought she ought to be doing herself. Since they were extremely poor, she really needed to be a good manager, but she was not. Mrs. Ramsay continued to help her even though she, too, gossiped about the Dempsters. Sometimes she left food for them while other times she tried to teach Mrs. Dempster the arts of housekeeping. Because Mrs. Dempster seemed unable to understand what she ought to do and because she played with her baby like a doll, even forgetting to cover herself after nursing him, people were convinced more than ever that she was simple. Furthermore, she didn't seem to value material possessions. On one occasion, she gave away a vase that the church had provided as part of the furnishings for their house. On other occasions, she gave food and money to tramps.

The Dempsters became more or less permanent charges of the Ramsays, a situation which meant that Dunny had certain jobs to do. His older brother Willie was not involved much because he was working at his father's newspaper in his spare time. But his mother sent Dunny to erase the chalk signs tramps left on the veranda posts to let other tramps know they could get something there. He also did odd jobs such as chopping wood, and tried to keep an eye on the baby for fear Mrs. Dempster might neglect him. As an adolescent with sexual curiosity, Dunny was not reluctant to help the Dempsters, for he could sometimes see Mrs. Dempster carelessly exposed after feeding the baby.

Commentary

In this chapter, Davies gives more information about the town in terms that are vivid and appropriate. There are a number of expressions which are typical of the people of Deptford and which make the town and its people come to life. For the most part, they use cliches like "hit the nail on the head," "show her the ropes" and "eating crow." But Davies invents some expressions himself which help make his style vital and original. He describes Mrs. Ramsay, for example, as a woman "who had strong features and stood for no nonsense from her hair." Mrs. Dempster, in contrast, is described by Mrs. Ramsay as having a "face like a pan of milk."

These two women represent two opposing sets of values for Dunstan. His mother is a woman of authority and order. Mrs. Dempster, on the other hand, is submissive and disorganized.

CHAPTER 6

Summary

Helping the Dempsters made Dunny unpopular at school.

Others talked behind his back about it, although no one said much to his face because he was big and strong for his age.

Percy Boyd Staunton was one of those who gossiped. He was as big as Dunny and quite plump. He wore better clothes than everyone else and had many possessions, such as an interesting pocketknife, and had once been to Toronto to the Exhibition. For these reasons, he seemed more important than the other boys. He and Dunny were rivals. Although Dunny could not compete with his wealth and elegant style, he was good at making sarcastic remarks or "good ones." He knew that Percy's mother had a pet nickname — Pidgy Boy-Boy — for him, and that if Percy ever bothered him about the Dempsters, he could retaliate by revealing the nickname.

Nevertheless, his responsibilities at the Dempsters' made life difficult for him. Not only did he have a double set of chores to do which left him little time to play, but also Mrs. Dempster's public displays of gratitude embarrassed him deeply and caused the other children to nickname him "Nursie."

Then there was the problem of girls at school. Dunny wanted them to like and admire him, especially Leola Cruikshank, but his feelings for Mrs. Dempster got in the way. Oddly enough, the stranger Mrs. Dempster became and the more other people looked down on her, the more Dunny became obsessed with her. Although he thought at the time that he was in love with Leola, he realized, looking back, that he had actually been in love with Mrs. Dempster. This bond was not a juvenile crush in which he worshipped from afar, but a combination of being in her company every day and feeling responsibility for her condition.

Dunny felt that he must defend her against the insults of others. When Milo Papple, the son of Myron Papple, the village barber, once told the others that Dunny could not play ball after school because he had to "get right over to the bughouse and cut the grass," Dunny got off a "good one" at Milo's expense. Since Milo was famous at school for making rude jokes and noises, Dunny responded in Mrs. Dempster's defence by saying "if you ever say that again, I'll get a great big cork and stick it up you, and then nobody'll ever laugh at you again." Although this tactic shut Milo up for the time being, Dunny sensed that others said the same kinds of things behind his back, and he felt more alone and closer to the Dempsters than ever before.

Commentary

The plot is advanced as Dunny's responsibilities to the Dempsters determine his relationship to his peer group. Instead of being one of the boys, he is marked out as a rather peculiar child because of his association with Mrs. Dempster. He is not so odd, however, that he cannot mix easily with his classmates. Percy, now becoming an important figure because of his wealth and wider experience, considers him a serious rival. But, whereas many girls send valentines to Percy on February 14th, only one girl sends Dunny one. For the first time, the question of love arises. Dunny is attracted to Leola Cruikshank, but his erotic attachment to Mrs. Dempster keeps him from pursuing girls his own age.

Consistent with Davies' earlier picture of Dunny, he is an observant and clever boy, who has turned these traits to his own advantage through well-aimed sarcasm. He still keeps his emotions under careful control, finding in Mrs. Dempster a safe outlet.

CHAPTER 7

Summary

Dunny was now 13 and was expected to help out at his father's newspaper as his brother Willie had. Unfortunately, he was a nuisance there because he had none of the skills necessary to the printing business. He was clumsy, messy and he couldn't read things upside down or backward. So his father found him another job as under-librarian three afternoons a week.

Dunny liked this job, even though he was not paid anything. It allowed him to have authority over other children when they came in to use the books. It even gave him the opportunity once to find something in an encyclopedia for Leola Cruikshank. Mostly, however, he had the place to himself, and he took advantage of this situation.

It was a small library which contained some odd things because most of the books came as gifts from the estates of people who had died. Consequently, there were some books which were kept in a locked closet off the main room: a medical book, for example, which had pictures of a fallen womb, a variocele and one of a man who had lost his nose through syphilis. The books that most interested Dunny were about magic:

The Secrets of Stage Conjuring by Robert-Houdin, and *Modern Magic* and *Later Magic* by Professor Hoffmann. By studying them, Dunny hoped to become a magician and impress his friends, especially Leola.

Dunny loved these books. To him, they seemed to present a world more real than the everyday life of Deptford. Reading of the many adventures of Robert-Houdin, Dunny imagined himself becoming a famous magician. He rejected the down-to-earth Scottish practicality of his parents in favour of this new vision of reality, even though he knew that most of the things necessary to becoming a successful magician — supplies, elegant clothes and an audience — were things he would never find in Deptford. He chose to study the only type of magic that needed no special equipment: the sleight-of-hand tricks of the classical *prestidigitateur*.

He began by practising with an egg he stole from his mother's kitchen, producing it from his mouth, elbow, knees and ears. After a fit of giggles, imagining what the magistrate would say if he had dared to try producing it from the man's beard as he took out a magazine from the library, he accidentally stuck his thumb through the egg when it was in his pocket.

His mother caught him trying to wash the pocket. Unfortunately, when interrogated, Dunny got off a "good one" at her expense and she became furious. She got out the pony whip with which she beat the boys when they misbehaved, and struck him over the left shoulder. "Don't you dare touch me," Dunny shouted, which put her into an even greater rage. She chased him around the kitchen hitting him with the whip until he cried. Then she cried too and beat him even harder until her fury lessened. Finally, she went upstairs in tears and slammed the door of her bedroom.

Dunny went out to the woodshed feeling like a criminal and wondering what he would do with himself. Become a tramp? Hang himself? It was misery which he would never forget. When his father and Willie came home, Dunny was forced to beg his mother's pardon on his knees, promising to love her always. After a small supper, his mother put him to bed kindly, whispering "I know I'll never have another anxious moment with my own dear laddie." Dunny could not figure out how his mother could be in a raging fury one minute and kindly and motherly the next. He concluded that nobody was to be trusted at face value.

Commentary

This chapter shows Dunny becoming more and more his real self instead of the person his parents — especially his mother — want him to be. Because he is clumsy, he doesn't fit into the family printing business. Because he is imaginative and a "loner" he can no longer accept the Scottish practicality his parents have tried to instil in him. Because he finds himself alone with books so much, and because he feels helpless to control a world in which his mother is so powerful, he has fantasies of power that center on magic. If he can learn to do magic tricks, he will impress everyone.

A break with his parents is almost accomplished in his fight with his mother. For the first time he stands up to her, realizing that she will not understand or approve of his new interest and aims. But she is an extremely powerful, dominating woman who will not tolerate any rebellion from her son. The cold reality of her fury makes her son deeply suspicious of the sincerity of her affection when she expresses it later. As he rightly senses, her affection is expressed in a way that reinforces her victory over his will, for she doesn't simply say that she cares about him, but says that she knows that she will not have any more trouble keeping him under her control. Here Davies portrays the point at which Dunny sees the difference between illusion and reality. His mother seems to love him, but really wants to control him. Ironically, the world of magic seems more real to him than his ordinary life, even though it consists of illusions and tricks.

CHAPTER 8

Summary

The fight with his mother made Dunny determined to gain power in some area his mother could not touch, so he continued practising magic tricks. Sometimes he felt positively about his mother, wanting her to love him and feeling sorry he had upset her. But, just as often, he had negative feelings, recognizing that she expected a lot in return for her affection.

Now he began to work on card tricks, using an old pack of cards his parents wouldn't miss. He got little Paul Dempster to be an audience for him, even though Paul was just four and he was 14. As a reward to keep Paul interested, he read to him from a book they both liked after each demonstration was finished. Even now, looking back, Dunny could remember an exact passage from this book — *A Child's Book of Saints* — and he quotes it to show the Headmaster what the book was like. The passage concerns a conversation between a little girl and her father about God's omniscience. She tells her father that she longs for Christ to come back to earth again, for she is certain he would be well-treated now under the protection of Queen Victoria. Dunny thought the writing in this book was elegant and beautiful.

So, for several months, Paul and Dunny met regularly at the library, Paul acting as a model audience in return for readings from the book. During this time, Dunny moved on from card tricks to coin tricks but found that his hands were too clumsy to become really good at it. Once, when he was doing a trick called "The Spider," Paul took the coin from him and did it perfectly, much better than Dunny could ever have done it. From that point on, Dunny became Paul's teacher, showing him how to do many tricks.

Paul was an odd-looking little boy with a large head and a frail body. Because his mother was such an unskilled housekeeper, his clothes were always ragged and badly fitted. His brown hair was thick and curly, much longer than other children's, because she refused to take him to the barber. His face was so pale that Mrs. Ramsay, thinking there must be something wrong, occasionally gave him medicine for worms. Paul was not much liked in the village, mainly because his mother was considered so peculiar.

Commentary

Here Dunny plays clearly the role of Fifth Business in relation to the much younger Paul Dempster. Although it is Dunny who is keen to become a magician, he has not the necessary skill with his hands to become successful. On the other hand, Paul Dempster has unusually clever hands, and although he is only supposed to be an audience for Dunny, he is the one who learns to do the tricks well.

Ironically, the method Dunny uses to reward Paul — reading stories about saints to him — will have far more effect on Dunny than on Paul. He is the one who will go on to make a lifetime study of the saints, while Paul will become a professional magician.

CHAPTER 9

Summary

Dunny disliked Amasa Dempster. He thought that he prayed too often and too emotionally. When Dunny was there helping, Reverend Dempster dropped to his knees, told Dunny to kneel too and then prayed for as long as 10 or 15 minutes. He asked God to prevent Dunny from making jokes to amuse Mrs. Dempster, and he would ask for the strength to tolerate living with his wife. But this was his only unkindness to her. Usually he was very patient.

Dunny realized that Reverend Dempster was not intelligent, but that he was extremely emotional. One day this emotion was directed at Dunny. He called him into his study in the church where they first knelt and prayed. Then Reverend Dempster accused him of corrupting childhood. At first Dunny thought that he meant the secret thoughts and feelings he had about sex, but it was his friendship with Paul that the Reverend was referring to. He was angry because Dunny was playing cards with Paul, an activity that Baptists thought sinful. He was also angry that Dunny was reading stories about the saints to Paul because saints were associated with the Roman Catholic church and were not a part of Baptist belief.

Reverend Dempster gave Dunny the choice between taking a beating from him for these evil deeds or having the Reverend tell the Ramsays about what their son had done. Dunny chose the latter, adding that he should also talk to their minister, the Presbyterian Reverend Andrew Bowyer. Dunny knew this was clever because no Presbyterian — either his parents or their minister — would have agreed with Dempster's idea that playing cards and reading about saints was evil. Dempster realized this and simply ordered him never to come near any of his family again.

This event upset Dunny and made him think about what religion meant to him. He did not think he had done wrong, although he blamed himself for forgetting how much Baptists hated cards. To him, his magic tricks seemed like the creation of a "world of wonders." As for the stories, he thought that they were tales of wonders just like *Arabian Nights*. In fact, he thought *Arabian Nights* and the Bible were similar. He would now look down on Amasa Dempster bitterly. He thought he was a petty, unimaginative man. He decided he would never be like that. He begged God to punish Dempster.

Dempster never did speak to Dunny's parents or the minister. When Dunny saw him, he seemed thinner and crazier than ever. When Dunny met Paul, Paul cried and ran home. As for Mrs. Dempster, she had begun to wander around absentmindedly giving away wilted things from her garden. Mrs. Ramsay pretended to be grateful and continued to help Mrs. Dempster by giving her more important things in return. She saw Mrs. Dempster's need to give as a religious virtue. Dunny still felt guilty about her, especially when she once asked him why he never came to see her.

Commentary

This chapter shows new developments in the character of Dunny. The Reverend Amasa Dempster's anger forces Dunny to look carefully at the role of emotion in life. Like most Presbyterians, he values intellect and distrusts emotion. In Dempster's fervent prayers and unreasonable anger, he experiences the harm that blind emotion can cause. As he concludes, looking back, "it was my first encounter with the emotional power of popular thought."

He decides that he will never be like Dempster, for the man's emotional way of life has made him a narrow-minded man. It has blinded him to what Dunny now begins to see are the finer things in life: a sense of the wonders of the world, wonders that are an aspect of both magic and true religion.

CHAPTER 10

Summary

It was late Friday evening on the 24th of October when the village policeman and a couple of other men came to the Ramsays' house. They were organizing a search party to look for Mrs. Dempster who had disappeared. Mrs. Ramsay told Dunny that he could go along with his father while she went over to look after Paul. Dunny knew this meant that she considered him to be grown up.

Dunny went to get the flashlight from the new car Mr. Ramsay had daringly bought recently, and they all went to look in the gravel pit for Mrs. Dempster. When they got there, they found the village magistrate and about a dozen men already assembled.

The large gravel pit ran along the west end of the village. It belonged to the railway company who used gravel from it to repair their roadbeds. Dunny's mother hated it because sometimes small children got lost there and were hurt, and sometimes older boys used it as a place to meet girls like Mabel Heighington for sexual encounters. Most of all, it was disliked because tramps hid there after jumping off the trains. These men drank anything with alcohol in it and begged for food. People were frightened of them. Because the pit seemed like a kind of Protestant hell, Dunny, looking back, sees that it was partly the cause of his later interest in myths about good and evil. Their minister, Andrew Bowyer, had actually compared the pit to Gehenna, the valley outside Jerusalem where outcasts lived.

The policeman and the magistrate led the search party who went down into the pit, spread out into a line and proceeded to walk from one end towards the other. Suddenly, Dunny heard a noise in a clump of scrub bush and called out to his father who ran over quickly. Shining his flashlight on the ground, Mr. Ramsay exposed a tramp making love to Mrs. Dempster right at Dunny's feet. The policeman ran over and pointed a gun at the terrified tramp. Mrs. Dempster calmly explained that he was deaf. Reverend Amasa Dempster joined them, helped his wife up protectively and asked her why she had done this. Her reply became famous in Deptford: "He was very civil, 'Masa. And he wanted it so badly."

Mr. Dempster took her arm and walked her home. The policeman took the tramp to jail. Everyone else went home silently.

Commentary

Davies displays his talent for the creation of a dramatic scene in this chapter. Without wasting words, he alternates dialogue and description to present the scene quickly and memorably. He gives the sense that something unusual is happening by describing Mr. Ramsay's conversation with the men who come to the door as "some quiet muttering." He recreates the local accent, complete with bad grammar, when the policeman says, "Yep, been gone since after supper.

Reverend come home at nine and she was gone. Nowheres round the town, and now we're goin' to search the pit.'' By using unusual and strong words, he brings the whole scene to life. The tramp "gaped at us in terror,'' the tramps' gatherings in the pit are called "jungles,'' the flashlight casts a "bleak, flat light,'' the tramps begging at the door have a "dazed, stunned look.''

This vivid scene stays with the reader as the point at which Dunny changes from boyhood to manhood.

CHAPTER 11

Summary

Reverend Amasa Dempster refused to lay any charges against the tramp, so he was freed and warned never to return to Deptford. All the villagers wondered what would happen on Sunday when Dempster would have to preach. Other ministers made reference in their prayers to what had happened, and the Roman Catholic priest even said that the gravel pit should be closed down. What people could not understand was Mrs. Dempster's giving the tramp permission. Dr. McCausland said that she must have some brain damage which would undoubtedly get worse.

Amasa Dempster announced in his church that he was resigning. His resignation was accepted. The Ramsays quarrelled about this. Mr. Ramsay wanted to help the Dempsters, but Mrs. Ramsay, like all the village women, was outraged at Mrs. Dempster's behaviour and would not let her husband give them anything.

The person who made the most of what had happened was the foul-mouthed bum, Cece Athelstan. He enjoyed making fun of respectable women who passed his chair outside the village bar and used to yell insults based on what Mrs. Dempster had said at the gravel pit. Dunny wanted to stop Cece, but was unable to have any effect on him. He was able to shut up the other boys at school, however, who naturally were curious about what he had seen.

The Dempsters moved into a small cottage after leaving the parsonage. Some village people gave them furniture and money, and even Mr. Ramsay managed to give them something secretly. But when they moved in, Cece organized a "house-warming party." A gang with blackened faces went to their house at night making a lot of noise and shouting insults.

The shame he now endured changed Amasa for the worse, even though he did manage to find a job in the sawmill. Soon he looked like a scarecrow. It was rumoured that he kept his wife tied up in the cottage. Feeling sorry for her, Dunny sneaked over to the house, tapped on the window and was soon inside. He found that she made quite good sense when she talked and that she was lonely. Dunny began to visit her regularly, bringing her the newspaper and reading to her from it so that she would know what was going on in the world. He also did what he could for Paul who was usually there because he never played with other children. No one mentioned these visits to Amasa Dempster or to Mrs. Ramsay, for they would have been furious. To Dunny, these visits were important. He found Mrs. Dempster a wise woman with interesting thoughts and opinions. She was unlike most Deptford women in that she suffered her fate cheerfully and seemed not to care about the usual values of the village. From her, Dunny learned strange and wonderful things of the spirit. In fact, he found her extremely religious. Even being kept as she was in a harness did not make her depressed or angry. Soon Dunny regarded her as his closest friend and the source of all that he valued in life. However, he never could have asked her about the tramp. Because he could not understand the event, he simply considered it madness.

Commentary

This chapter highlights Davies' social criticism. He examines the values held by the people of Deptford and contrasts them to another set of values represented by Mrs. Dempster. The townspeople's values are closely tied in with their religious beliefs. Although there are several different religions represented in Deptford, all agree that what Mrs. Dempster has done is evil and wrong. She has committed adultery deliberately and thus has broken one of the ten commandments. The women especially are offended and will not allow their husbands to help the Dempsters get established again: "Any man who spoke up for Mary Dempster probably believed in Free Love. Certainly he associated sex with pleasure, and that put him in a class with filthy thinkers like Cece Athelstan." So great is the general condemnation, that it kills Amasa Dempster's spirit and forces him out of the job he loves. It is interesting to note that the townspeople show no Christian forgiveness and allow Cece Athelstan and his gang to indulge in cruel jests at the Dempsters' expense.

In contrast to this hard, pleasure-denying religion, Mrs. Dempster represents another kind of religious nature. She is religious both in her attitude and her example. No matter how much she is hurt and joked about, she remains cheerful and generous. Her ideas are broad in outlook and her vision of life is clear. The kind of religion she represents "enriches" Dunny, who finds his life greatly enhanced by conversations with her. Through her, he defines his view of life against the one in which he has been raised.

CHAPTER 12

Summary

The following year was lonely for Dunny, except for his visits to Mrs. Dempster. His school friends called him a "know-all," a label he actually liked. Finding that the dictionary term for a know-all was a "polymath," he set out to make himself a real polymath by reading as much of the encyclopedia as he could. Eventually he gained enough information to be a nuisance to everyone.

He now became closer to his father, especially during long walks together along the railway on Sundays. His father was well-educated and encouraged him to study Latin so that he would write better English.

Sometimes the two of them were joined by an electrician who was an atheist. Although he did not believe in God, he had a thorough knowledge of the Bible and used to quote from it to demonstrate how foolish religion is. But Dunny continued to be religious himself because he saw that the Bible was really an imaginative work full of metaphors which appealed to him. Therefore, he thought it was useless to apply strict reason to it.

Mr. Ramsay was now Chairman of the Continuation School Board and Dunny began to act as if he were on the same level as the teachers. Looking back after teaching many similar students himself, Dunny admits that he was very tiresome.

Ramsay's other friends were also growing up. Leola was now a beauty and had been claimed by Percy as his girlfriend. Milo Papple had developed his rude jokes to include more adult material.

The great scandal of that spring occurred when Mabel Heighington's mother discovered her having intercourse with Percy. She went straight to Dr. Staunton and demanded that he do something to make up for her daughter's supposed loss of virtue. It was rumoured that he paid her 50 or 100 dollars. Dr. Staunton, by this time, had become extremely wealthy by building up his property to include a lot of land where tobacco and sugar beets were grown. He continued his medical practice because it gave him prestige, but his real interest was now in these properties. As a result of the scandal about his son, he sent Percy away to a private school, Colborne College.

Commentary

Davies skillfully treats the passage of time in this chapter. Although it is a short chapter, he makes a year pass before the reader's eyes. Dunny says that the year was "a busy one," and he goes on to give only the highlights of the year rather than everything that happened. Davies allows the reader to gain information about changes that have taken and are taking place in Dunny and his classmates. They have all grown into young men and women with many of the same characteristics they had as children. Leola is the most desirable girl, Milo the rude joker, Percy the self-indulgent rich boy. Dr. Staunton has gained more wealth — enough to send his son away to an expensive private school. Dunny emerges as an intellectual during this year. Proud to be called a "know-all," he turns his attention to acquiring knowledge, a development which brings him closer to his father who can now discuss things man-to-man with him.

CHAPTER 13

Summary

Deptford remembered the fall of 1914 not only because the war broke out, but because Dunny's brother, Willie, became ill. He had been sick on and off for four years, ever since he had an accident at the newspaper plant. One of the big rollers had fallen on him, knocking him down and bruising his back. He began to have unexplained periods of illness with internal pain. Usually he got better after a few days in bed, but that fall he began experiencing delirium and could not urinate. A Toronto specialist was called in who recommended that Willie be put in warm water every four hours.

The village people supplied many willing helpers to assist with this task. Even Cece Athelstan turned up surprisingly sober and the new Presbyterian minister helped too. These baths made Willie feel better, but he was swollen more than ever from the retention of urine.

After two weeks of this treatment, on the Saturday of the Fall Fair, Dunny was left to look after Willie because his father had to judge some events and his mother had to organize the Fowl Supper. While they were gone, Willie had a convulsion, grew very cold and died. Dunny couldn't hear a heartbeat, nor could he see any signs of breathing when he held a mirror close to Willie's mouth. When he pulled open one eye, it was rolled upward.

Dunny panicked and, instead of calling the doctor, he raced over to fetch Mrs. Dempster whose cottage was only three minutes away. He climbed in through a window, cut the rope that held her, dragged her back out the window behind him and the two of them raced back to Willie's bedside. Mrs. Dempster knelt and prayed, then raised her head and called Willie quietly and cheerfully by name. Dunny looked on, hoping against hope that Willie would revive. Finally Willie sighed and moved a little. Dunny fainted.

When he regained consciousness, he found Willie and Mrs. Dempster talking quietly together. Soon the men came to give Willie his six o'clock bath. Though they were surprised to see Mrs. Dempster there, they were polite. Eventually, the Ramsays came home with Amasa Dempster. He took his wife's arm and led her home. Mrs. Dempster blew Willie a kiss goodbye — something Dunny had never seen before — and Willie blew one back to her. Dunny thought this a beautiful gesture. Mrs. Ramsay looked furious.

The Ramsays were enraged at Dunny. Why had he not called the doctor? Why had he not come to get them? Why had he allowed that insane woman near Willie? Was he out of his mind too? How did he know Mrs. Dempster so well anyway?

In the middle of their tirade, Dr. McCausland arrived and inquired about what had happened. He refused to believe that Willie had died. He said that Dunny must have been wrong because he was young and inexperienced. He said that Willie's hands were clenched because of a convulsion, not because he was dead.

The next day, Dr. McCausland returned and "tapped"

Willie, inserting a needle into his side and taking out a large quantity of bloody urine. In a week, Willie was well again. Four months later he lied about his age to get into the army. In 1916 he disappeared forever at the battle at St. Eloi in France.

Dunstan, looking back, wondered if Willie's hands were clenched in death. Certainly, many soldiers he later saw dead on the battlefield had clenched hands, though he never told Dr. McCausland about it. To him, Willie's return from the dead was Mrs. Dempster's second miracle.

Commentary

This chapter is notable for its dramatic presentation of what Dunny calls "Mrs. Dempster's second miracle." Davies gives us a detailed and action-packed description of this striking event. Mrs. Dempster, for example, runs to Willie's bedside with her skirts "hoisted up" and Dunny notes that this was "a girlish thing no grown woman would ever have done if she had not caught the infection of my emotion." Dunny's feelings, upon concluding that his brother had died, are aptly described as "the psychological equivalent of a house falling in upon itself." Much of Dr. McCausland's character and a good deal of Dunny's dislike of him is summed up in the sentence: "He brought his own sort of atmosphere, which was cold and chilly and smelled of disinfectant, and took a good look at Willie." The whole section remains vividly in the reader's mind because of small touches like these which enable the reader to visualize clearly what is happening and to feel intensely the high pitch of emotion Dunny himself feels.

CHAPTER 14

Summary

The weeks that followed Willie's recovery were painful to Dunny. Friends he had impressed by being a polymath now thought he was stupid to have believed a dangerous lunatic like Mrs. Dempster could raise anyone from the dead. It now became obvious that Dunny had been visiting her secretly, which gave rise to many dirty jokes at his expense.

Adults in the town took the matter more seriously. They wondered whether Dunny had been studying so hard that he had "brain fever." Some thought he should leave school for a while to work on a farm. Dr. McCausland told him that he'd better acquire some common sense to balance his intellectual knowledge. The new minister told him that it was blasphemy to believe that anyone could bring the dead to life: "The age of miracles was past." Dunny could see that he meant well, which Dr. McCausland certainly didn't.

Mr. Ramsay told Dunny that he should do what his mother wanted. Mrs. Ramsay brought up the subject so often that she made Dunny feel rebellious. Although he loved her, he realized that the only kind of love she recognized was loyalty, and to be loyal to her meant betraying things he deeply believed in. After all, he was not her husband who might compromise for the sake of peace at home. He was her son, and, in some ways, he resembled her for he also had a temper and strong willpower.

Finally, Mrs. Ramsay demanded that he choose between herself and Mrs. Dempster. Dunny decided on something else; he chose to leave home and enlist in the army. Although he was two years under age, he lied and was accepted. His father prevented his mother from taking him out of the army, but he was disgusted with his son. He disliked war and urged Dunny to withdraw, but Dunny was stubborn and wouldn't change his mind. In fact, he boasted about it at school while he waited to be called into action. Now, he was more attractive to Leola who told him she loved him more than Percy, who didn't bother to write much to her from his school. Before leaving, Dunny went to say goodbye to Mrs. Dempster. She told him never to be afraid. Eventually his call came, and he took the train to the army camp.

Commentary

This concludes the Deptford section of the novel and sums up many things Davies has introduced to this point. Dunny is now fully a man, making his own decisions and breaking ties with his family, especially with his mother who has done her best to control his life. It is now clear that Dunny cannot remain in Deptford. His values, fostered mainly by his friendship with Mrs. Dempster, are quite different from those of the village in which he has grown up. Intellectually, he is superior to his friends, and his interest in having a wider life can never be satisfied if he stays in Deptford. For all these reasons, Davies makes it seem inevitable that Dunny will take advantage of the event which has caused so much trouble at home — his insistence that

Mrs. Dempster has raised his brother from the dead — to leave Deptford at the first opportunity. The romantic notion of war, mainly a result of being so far removed from what was really happening on the battlefield, provides that opportunity.

PART TWO • CHAPTER 1

Summary

Dunstable says little about the war in which he took part from 1915 to late 1917 because he didn't find out much about it until later. Since he was in the infantry, he only followed orders and couldn't tell what was going on. At the training camp he was homesick and lonely. None of his fellow-soldiers had any education or any idea of geography or history. Dunstable was in the Second Canadian Division, later part of the Canadian Corps. Although he would like to have had friends in the army, he didn't meet anyone he liked well enough to form a lasting friendship with.

Above all, he was bored because he felt cut off from the things that make life interesting and pleasant. For the most part, all he did was repetitive jobs that helped him learn skills he didn't especially want to have.

When he went home on leave, he impressed everyone because he had grown up and become a man. Even his mother was a bit intimidated by him, though she tried unsuccessfully to treat him at times as her little boy. Leola was proud to be seen with him. He could not visit Mrs. Dempster, however, because he was conspicuous in his uniform and everyone would know if he did. He was still a bit afraid of his mother.

Eventually, he went off on a boat to France, having been told how dreadful the Germans were. There he was no longer bored, but afraid. Although he saw many others break down under the strain, he was strong and was not injured. He experienced all the horrors of war: fear of being trampled by horses, fear of being shot, disgust at the many corpses underfoot and also pity for the wounded who longed for death. The greatest danger occurred when there was not much action. Then the soldiers would lose their sense of themselves and needed to be sent back to rest camps.

In spite of the fact that everything the soldiers did was public, Dunstable found some time for reading alone. The only book he had was the New Testament. He would rather have had some long novels or even the Old Testament, but having no choice, he read what he had. He read it over and over. The others concluded that he was very religious, when, in fact, he was only curious. They nicknamed him "Deacon." Revelation was his favourite book of the New Testament, mainly because

41

he liked the visions John had of the beasts and the struggle which the Crowned Woman with the moon beneath her feet had with the great Red Dragon. His reading made him more certain than ever that religion and *Arabian Nights* were true in the same way. Looking back, he could say what he could not have put into words then, that the two were psychologically, rather than literally, true.

One evening, his nickname changed from Deacon to "Charlie." There was a show at a rest camp in which soldiers were asked to put on an act. Dunstable did a good imitation of Charlie Chaplin and told a lot of rude jokes the way Milo Papple used to in Deptford. The soldiers loved his act and were truly surprised that the man they had thought was so religious could come out with such vulgar and funny jokes. Dunstable was equally amazed at their surprise.

Eventually he became a sergeant and fought and survived the battles of Sanctuary Wood and Vimy Ridge before he was 20. But his greatest achievement during this time, in his opinion, was being "Charlie."

Commentary

In his account of the war, Ramsay points to the difference between the surface appearance of things and the reality that lies beneath the surface. To the world at large, the war is a glorious endeavour made up of heroic battles. But the reality which Dunstable experiences as a common soldier is something quite different. The main problem is boredom, not fighting. Many of the soldiers have no idea what kind of climate to expect in France let alone why the war is being fought or what the overall plan of attack is. What seemed real to Ramsay, at the time, was not the official aspects of army life, such as the name of the division he belonged to, but the daily life of the common soldier with its lack of privacy, its loneliness and its occasional times of fun like the show in which he imitates Charlie Chaplin. Although from the outside, to people like his parents and Leola, he may appear to be an impressive and even heroic figure, he actually thinks the skills that have made him a presentable soldier are easy to acquire and insignificant. He is thought to have a "cool head" and for this reason is promoted to the rank of sergeant. Inside, however, he is not cool at all, but simply good at hiding his fear.

CHAPTER 2

Summary

Ramsay's last battle in the war took place during the Third Battle of Ypres when the Canadian troops were brought in to try to take Passchendaele in November, 1917. It was the most terrible battle in his experience. They were trying to take a ruined village, and advanced very slowly towards it because of the muddy ground. One night it was Ramsay's turn, along with five other soldiers, to try to take a German emplacement of machine gun operators. As they crawled toward the emplacement, the Germans sent up flares which showed where Ramsay and the others were. As a couple of the flares were hissing down over Ramsay, he knew he must make a dash for safety or be hit and burned. With shells falling around him, he dashed wildly about until he saw, in a burst of light, a partly concealed entry. In he went, saw three Germans in front of him firing guns, raised his revolver and shot them. He was not proud of himself; he simply did what had to be done. Knowing he was in danger if he stayed in the German emplacement, he began to crawl across the mud which was full of dead and dying soldiers. Frightened and confused, he was hit by a fragment of exploding shell in the left leg and seriously wounded.

Dragging his helpless left leg along, he crawled as best he could up to a partly ruined stone wall. This moment, in which he knew he would probably die, was the low point of his life. His leg began to pain him terribly and he was convinced that even if he were spared now, he would get tetanus and die. He thought of Deptford and of Mrs. Dempster. He remembered her last words of advice, "whatever happens, it does no good to be afraid." But he did feel afraid and could not help it. Then something extraordinary happened. It was something that Packer would never understand or believe. The battle stopped, and he realized that he was leaning against the ruined tower of a large building — perhaps a church or a school. Looking up in the light of a flare, he could see a statue of the Virgin and Child above him. Looking back, he realized that it was a representation of the Immaculate Conception. At the time, he thought it was the Crowned Woman in Revelation which he had enjoyed reading about in the New Testament. But the remarkable thing was that the face of the Virgin was exactly like that of Mrs. Dempster. Then he lost consciousness.

Commentary

Davies relies almost entirely on his descriptive powers to present the drama of this scene. Ramsay states that he wishes to keep the description brief because the terror of the incident was so great he does not wish to relive it.

By selecting a few vivid details, however, Davies is able to recreate the horror of the event. He compares crawling across the mud, for example, to "swimming in molasses, with the additional misery that it was molasses that stank and had dead men in it." Being hit with a piece of shell is "a sudden shock like a blow from a club." His description of the growing pain in his leg is especially vivid: "I can only describe it in terms of sound; from a mute condition it began to murmur, then to moan and whine, then to scream."

CHAPTER 3

Summary

When Ramsay gained consciousness he found himself in a special hospital in an old house in Buckinghamshire, England. It was the 12th of May. All he could remember of the six months that had passed was that he had been in a blissful state in which everything was good. His spirit was entirely his own. He recalled hearing the little Madonna he had seen just before he lost consciousness speak to him occasionally, but could not remember what she had said.

The nurse looking after him, Diana Marfleet, was a pretty, lively girl who had fair skin, and brown hair and eyes. She had been tending him all the time he lay unconscious. His left leg had been amputated. Because he had to be force fed, he was very thin. But he felt wonderful and enjoyed joking with Diana, whose fiancé had been lost at sea during the war.

One day Diana came in to tell him that he had been presumed dead and because his identification disks had been burned up when the flare he heard, just before losing consciousness, hit him. The flare had also caused bad burns on his chest and left side. Now that he had regained consciousness, however, he could remember his name and everything else that had happened. So the Victoria Cross (V.C.) that had been awarded to him posthumously could be presented to him in person. The medal was awarded to him for bravery in killing the three Germans.

44

A few days later, a letter arrived from the Reverend Donald Phelps in reply to the one the doctor had sent to the Ramsays in Deptford. This letter informed them that both Ramsay's parents had died in the influenza epidemic that had swept through Deptford in early 1918. They died, thinking that he had been killed at Passchendaele.

Commentary

This chapter provides a pleasing contrast to the one just before it. The difference in tone between the two chapters is emphatic. Whereas the previous scene is tense and terrible in depicting war, this scene is one of refreshing coolness and healing. Instead of the battlefield, the setting is a hospital in a pleasant part of England. Ramsay rejoices in the "sweet air" and the cleanliness of his surroundings, a marked contrast to his horror of the stench and mud of the battlefield in France.

His recovery is not merely a physical one, but also a spiritual one. In the previous chapter his "nerve dissolved" into a nightmarish vision of suffering and death. Now, he recalls the almost heavenly state in which he has lingered for six months. He compares it to a stanza from Coleridge's "Kubla Khan," a romantic poem which describes an imagined experience of being in Paradise. "Though everything was strange," he observes of his unconscious state, "nothing was evil." In symbolic terms, he has moved from the "hell" of the battlefield to the "heaven" of peace and healing in the English hospital.

Although it is understated and not emphasized, Davies indicates that it has been the little Madonna (who seemed to him to have the face of Mrs. Dempster), who has been Ramsay's spiritual guardian during this time.

CHAPTER 4

Summary

Ramsay felt only relief at his parents' death. Only much later would he be able to see them as real people who had done their best. But now, he was glad he would not have to conform to please his mother. He knew that she had dominated his father and had also wanted to dominate him, and it had been a struggle to keep her from doing so. He was even glad she would never know about his V.C. because she would just boast about it to others.

He became closer to Diana. The two of them were young and romantic. He told her all about Canada, even about Mrs. Dempster (though not about his guilt). When he told her about the little Madonna at Passchendaele, Diana interpreted it as a conventionally religious event, not the way Ramsay saw it all.

She often spoke about her parents whom she visited on her days off. Her father was an Anglican priest, Canon Marfleet, who was chaplain to the Royal Family at Windsor Castle, as well as having a parish of his own. Her mother was an English aristocrat of the De Blaquiere family. The family was rich. They had two servants and a gardener. This they considered "living very simply." They took daily baths, something Ramsay had never heard of before.

Diana began to correct Ramsay's speech and manners so that he would fit in with the better class of people from which she came. She did this gently and humorously. She also helped him learn to walk again with an artificial leg and crutches.

Eventually, she took him home to meet her parents. They were unlike any parents Ramsay had seen before: the Canon wanted to have intelligent and cultured conversations about the war (not about religion, as Ramsay expected); and the "Honourable" (as Ramsay thought of the mother) was beautiful and apparently scatterbrained, but actually intelligent. She was what Diana would be like at her age.

Ramsay enjoyed the whole experience of getting to know the Marfleets and their daughter. It was an education for him. Through them he entered a more sophisticated social and cultural world, learned good manners and expanded his spirit.

Commentary

Although Ramsay is attracted to Diana and enjoys her parents, Davies presents this episode in a way that conveys darker undertones to the reader. He begins with Ramsay's relief at his mother's death and his sense of freedom from her domination: "Oh, these good, ignorant, confident women! How one grows to hate them!" This generalization about women suggests that Ramsay will want to be cautious about getting involved with such a woman again. But, ironically, Davies gives many signs that Diana Marfleet is just such a woman, even though Ramsay himself cannot see it.

Diana is also "good" and "confident." Like Mrs. Ramsay, she enjoys the authority she has as a nurse helping others. While this is praiseworthy, it is also a sign that she likes to control. In fact, in her hands, Ramsay is her dependent inferior. In addition, Diana decides to "correct" Ramsay's speech and manners. "Confident" that her way is the right way, so confident that she can joke about it, she is imposing her will and her ways on him. Since Ramsay is eager to acquire these social skills, he is willing. But is he likely to want a lifetime partnership with someone who thinks she can tell him the right thing to do on all matters? Even the frivolous conversation of the beautiful Mrs. Marfleet is ominous. Ramsay correctly observes that Diana will be just like her mother, but he also observes that her mother is only pretending to be brainless in order to get her own way. Is Diana's "charm" the same? Because this chapter prepares for what happens to the relationship in Part Two, Chapter 6, it is a good example of the technique called foreshadowing.

CHAPTER 5

Summary

Ramsay was happy that the war was over for him, even though it was still going on. He simply rested and planned to learn to walk with a crutch at first, then with an artificial leg and a cane. Although not positively in love with Diana, he was charmed by her and flattered by her attention.

Finally, on November 11, 1918, the war was over. The doctor took Ramsay, another patient, Diana and another nurse into London to see the celebrations. Ramsay was upset at the noise and confusion and disgusted at the behaviour of the crowd who were destructive. That night, he slept with Diana at her aunt's house while the aunt was out. It was his first sexual experience. She was not a virgin and took the initiative in lovemaking. To Ramsay, this was an important step in completing his sense of manhood.

The next night, they went to see *Chu-Chin-Chow* at His Majesty's theater in London. This was Ramsay's first real cultural experience. He had tried to find Robert-Houdin's theater in Paris when on leave in France, forgetting that it had been there so long ago that it would not be there now. His historical sense would develop later.

Both events — his sexual initiation and his cultural initiation — were wonders for Ramsay.

The next great moment in his life occurred when King George V pinned the V.C. on him in a public ceremony at Buckingham Palace. Diana went with him. There he and the king looked into one another's eyes which was a revelation to Ramsay. At that moment, he realized he was acting the role of a hero (since he didn't really think his actions on the battlefield had been heroic) and the king was also acting the role of king (since he was king simply because he happened to be born into the right family). Such roles, Ramsay decided, require that people have responsibilities above what is merely personal: they must act out convincingly their public roles. This became even clearer to him at a lunch afterwards which the Canon and Mrs. Marfleet gave for Diana and himself. Ramsay did his best to behave like his idea of a public hero: modest, but not too modest. This experience made him sympathetic to people in public roles from then on.

Commentary

This chapter makes three strong points against Packer's summary of Ramsay's life. It reveals the importance of Ramsay's sexual, cultural and public initiation. He has made love to Diana Marfleet with deep emotion and pleasure; he has been enriched by his first taste of good theater in London and he has seen deep into the meaning of public responsibility at the time he received his V.C. All three are significant aspects of manhood to Ramsay, and all three have been overlooked in Packer's account of his life. If this chapter is compared to Packer's article in Part One, Chapter 2, it can be seen that experiences such as these — so important in the maturing of Ramsay — make Packer's portrait of Ramsay as a foolish old bachelor seem inaccurate.

CHAPTER 6

Summary

Ramsay found it difficult to get used to managing with his artificial leg and his damaged left arm because he was so clumsy.

Worse than that, he had to decide about Diana. He knew he would always be grateful to her for teaching him about physical love, and for making his life so pleasant while he got better from his war wounds, but he realized that she was too much like a mother to him. Certainly he had no intention of being dominated by a woman again. He decided that he would not marry her. From now on he would live the way he wanted to.

This decision was difficult to convey to Diana. She had decided that she and Ramsay would marry and go to Canada to live on a farm. At Christmas, which they spent with her parents, she raised the subject by asking about the letters Ramsay received every two weeks from Leola. Diana knew they were from a girl by the handwriting, and she was jealous.

Ramsay himself was perplexed about his relationship with Leola. After such a long time and so many experiences, not to mention his relationship with Diana, he was uncertain what to do about her. He didn't know, for example, whether Leola really loved him. As for himself, he now found her letters so stupid, dull and poorly-written that he imagined he did not really care about her.

However, he clumsily told Diana about Leola, and she began to cry. At first Diana accused him of thinking she was too old for him, though the four years' difference in their ages didn't bother Ramsay. Next, because Ramsay told her that he was not committed to Leola, she concluded wrongly that he must be committed to her. She urged him not to think, but to follow his feelings for her and get married. Though her tactics in this fight for Ramsay were crafty, he was also crafty in fighting for his freedom. The war had upset him, he argued, and he had no clear ideas yet about the future.

He made the mistake of saying that he could not expect her to marry a cripple. This gave her the chance to flatter him, saying that no decent woman would be bothered by the evidence of a man's courage and sacrifice for his country. This flattery, more than any of her other arguments, almost persuaded him to give in. He was disgusted that he liked being flattered.

Finally, Diana gave in, seeing that she could not get him. However, she was a good loser and became his friend afterwards. She asked what Ramsay would do with his life, this time with a genuine concern. But Ramsay could not tell her that he wished to pursue the question of the little Madonna because he knew Diana would not see it the same way he did. So he told her that he planned to go to university in Canada to improve his education, which was true.

Diana insisted on re-naming him. His name had been

Dunstable, his mother's maiden name. She persuaded him to change it to the better-sounding Dunstan. St. Dunstan was a marvellous person who she felt was very similar to Ramsay: keen on learning, stern and stubborn. When the Devil once came to tempt him in the form of a fascinating woman, St. Dunstan took her nose in his goldsmith's tongs and gave it a hard twist. The newly-named Dunstan then took her nose and gave it a twist, which made her a little angry.

The Marfleets were glad that Diana had decided not to marry him. They thought the two were too different in background.

Commentary

This chapter resolves the tensions raised in Chapter 4. Diana, despite her charm, is a serious and clever opponent with "a great gift for getting her own way." Now Ramsay sees through her pretty appearance and light-hearted ways to the real forcefulness of her personality. He recognizes that she is too much like his mother for him to be happily married to her. In fact, his description of her nursing skills sounds exactly like the role a mother plays in relation to a baby and growing child.

> I could not be blind to the fact that she regarded me as her own creation. And why not? Hadn't she fed me and washed me and lured me back into this world when I was far away? Didn't she teach me to walk, showing the greatest patience when I was most clumsy? Was she not also anxious to retrain me about habits of eating and behaviour? (p. 80)

He sees now that she has been raised to believe in "the emotional superiority of womanhood," and he has no intention of letting her dominate him. Diana's final gesture is also "motherly," for she "baptizes" him with her father's port and gives him a new name.

As with his mother, however, the fight is a close one, and he almost gives in when she flatters him. But his instinct for freedom and the need to direct his own life prove stronger than her feminine tactics.

Davies cleverly uses the language of a battle to show that here, as on the real battlefield in France, Ramsay is fighting for his life. Diana's methods of arguments are "tactics". She claims he is "throwing" an insult "in her face" and Ramsay calls his explanations about Leola "verbal acrobatics" that lead into "a blazing row."

CHAPTER 7

Summary

Ramsay returned to Deptford where he was given a hero's welcome. The reeve met him and drove with him in an open car at the head of a procession which included people dressed in costumes to represent figures in the war. The shoe-repair man was Marshall Foch, Myron Papple was the German Emperor, there were two John Bulls (by mistake), several Red Cross nurses and a girl with big feet dressed as Gallant Little Belgium. Although Ramsay could see how funny this procession was, he knew that it was meant as a tribute to him and he was pleased.

He was given a room at the Tecumseh Hotel where he had to stay out of sight until the formal ceremony, which began with a dinner at the reeve's house. Ramsay spent some time reading *War and Peace*, one of the novels he wished he had had at the Front during the war.

After a large cold buffet dinner with lots of coffee, he and the other guests proceeded to the Athelstan Opera House in the main business section of Deptford where the awards and speeches would be made. There was a stage party of several town dignitaries. Ramsay was the only soldier among them. But there were six other soldiers in the front row with the audience. One of them was Percy Boyd Staunton, now a major, sitting next to Leola who was wearing a large diamond engagement ring. Ramsay was pleased that he would not have any problem with Leola, but he was also annoyed that she had not written to tell him.

The hall was decorated with flags and other patriotic banners. The ceremony began with *God Save the King* and *The Maple Leaf Forever*. Solos were performed, poetry was read, a child played the piano and a local wit told riddles and jokes. Then Father Regan read the names of the eleven men from Deptford, including Willie, who had died in the war. Next the M.P. gave a long speech. The reeve also made a speech, and then he and the M.P. presented engraved railway watches to each of the men from Deptford who had survived the war. Ramsay watched jealously while Percy Boyd Staunton made a stylish salute to the audience after receiving his watch. Ramsay was last. He was given special recognition by being seated onstage. The ceremony ended with *God Save the King*.

Afterwards, Ramsay went up to congratulate Percy and kiss Leola. Percy announced his engagement loudly, to which Ramsay replied "Well, well, the best man has won!" and kissed Leola again. He thoroughly enjoyed the drama of this moment. He knew that the three of them made an interesting love triangle to all the spectators. But inside he was annoyed at Percy, as he had always been, and though he did not want Leola himself, he resented Percy's having her. The three of them went off to watch the bonfire. Myron Papple, still in costume, played the role of the German tyrant. "Hang him!" called out the crowd in a mounting frenzy. Over the bonfire, an effigy of the emperor, which quickly replaced Myron Papple, was tied up above the flames and burned.

Ramsay, who remembered all too well what it actually felt like to be severely burned, was appalled to see his own village people turn into a hysterical crowd delighting in cruelty and hatred. He left early, the acted-out screams of Myron Papple ringing in his ears.

Commentary

Davies uses descriptive style in this passage for humorous effect. The procession through town consists of "people dressed in patriotic but vague outfits," which suggest they don't know much about the war or history generally. The procession is led by "seven brass instruments and a thunderous drum," hardly a polished military band! The buffet offers "pickles in bewildering variety." The theater curtain at the Athelstan Opera House is painted with "a sort of composite view, or evocation, of all that was romantic in Europe," even though a scene containing gondaliers, large ships, castles and snow-capped mountains could never have existed anywhere in the same place. The scenery at the back of the stage "portrayed a dense and poisonously green forest," the soloist "shrieked" her songs. Thus Davies satirizes the cultural and aesthetic ignorance of small town people of the time in Canada.

Davies' satire here, however, is made gentler by Ramsay's situation. Although he knows that "Deptford's version of a Roman triumph" is ridiculous, he doesn't laugh at it because he knows it is not their fault that they don't know any better. In fact, they want to show him how much they value what he has done, and he does his best to be worthy of it.

CHAPTER 8

Summary

The next day, Ramsay went over to his parents' house which looked much the same, but neglected. He picked up a few things, especially something he had kept hidden for a long time, and left quickly.

He visited Willie's old girl friend, who remembered his brother as her first lover. But the main thing about Willie for Ramsay was that he had died twice and that it had been Mrs. Dempster who had brought him back to life the first time.

Ramsay went to get a haircut at Papple's, where he found Milo had almost completely taken over the business from his father. Milo's gossip — mainly stories about sexual misdoings, disasters and death, brought Ramsay up-to-date on what had happened in Deptford in his absence. He learned about Percy's courtship of Leola as soon as he finished school at Colborne College. He also heard all about the flu epidemic in which his mother and father died. Ninety-eight of the 500 people in Deptford had died. Dr. McCausland worked day and night to help, but Doc Staunton gave up his practice and avoided the danger by moving to one of his farms. Ramsay also learned that Mrs. Dempster had been taken away by her aunt to live in Weston, near Toronto. She became much worse after Paul ran away at the age of nine to join a circus, and when Amasa died soon afterwards of the flu.

On Sunday, Ramsay went to the Presbyterian Church. On Monday, he left Deptford by train, though he would realize later that he never entirely left it in spirit.

Commentary

Davies skillfully uses the barber, Milo Papple, for several purposes at the same time. First of all, Milo's non-stop chatter gives authentic local colour to the scene. Expressions like "went clean off her head," "Isn't that a corker, eh?" and "Jeez the war's made a difference in this little old burg." are realistic representations of the way a person like Milo would have talked. Furthermore, the speech is filled with humour. Milo is a comical character even when he does not intend to be.

Davies also mixes information which is important to Ramsay with matters of no significance whatsoever. Thus, Ramsay can catch up on what he has missed during his absence, though he must choose what interests him from the stream of gossip. Davies also gives a sense of time passing and the changes that have taken and are taking place in Deptford: the war has had an impact on village life, and morality is freer, for example. Finally, Davies gives the reader the information he needs to fill in bits of the plot that have been missing, such as how Leola became engaged to Percy, and information the reader will need later, such as Mrs. Dempster's move to Weston, in order to conclude Part Two of the novel.

PART THREE • CHAPTER 1

Summary

In the fall of 1919, Ramsay entered University College at the University of Toronto in the Honours History program. He was given special permission to enrol because he was a veteran.

Ramsay was wealthy enough to pay for the four years it took him to get a B.A., and also for another year to get an M.A. He had sold his parents' house for $1200 and its contents for $600. He had also sold his father's newspaper business for $750 down and $2750 in installments over four years (though he never got all of this amount). He had a good pension for his disabilities, and an annual $50 for the V.C. During the summers he took easy jobs that gave him some time to read, and he earned enough money to live on without touching his capital.

Ramsay enjoyed the study of history, especially one branch of history which involved his intelligence. He graduated first in his class. He also studied many subjects that gave him a "rounded" education: zoology, French and Religious Knowledge. But he was quite lonely and didn't make any close friends. He was not at his best as a young man.

On the other hand, Percy Boyd Staunton, who now called himself Boy Staunton, was a dashing young man. He was typical of that era: he was handsome, a good dancer; he looked like a movie star or an F. Scott Fitzgerald character and he modelled himself after the charming Edward, Prince of Wales. Boy was in law school, not because he intended to be a lawyer, but because law school would give him prestige and a good preparation for business and politics. He had a knack for making money, like his father. Doc Staunton had made a lot of money out of his sugar beet crops. Boy took the family enterprise a step further by persuading his father to buy into the secondary industries involved in the manufacture of sugar from the beets. Boy also made some good investments in the stock market which enabled him to indulge his taste for high living and expensive things.

Ramsay envied Boy's financial success and was critical of his life generally. However, he was not above letting Boy advise him how to invest some of his own money, knowing that he could make some money from Boy's financial expertise.

The two men were actually very different. Boy was interested only in external things: money, objects, girls he could have fun with and alcohol. For Ramsay, reality lay in things spiritual or things of the mind. Nonetheless, they met every couple of weeks to talk. Usually they spoke about Leola. The Cruikshanks had insisted that Boy must wait to marry Leola until he had finished law school.

When Boy visited Leola on occasional weekends, they had frequent sexual encounters that stopped just short of actual intercourse. Thus Leola remained, technically, a virgin. But this was not enough for Boy, who found a variety of girls in the city who were not so careful. This led to guilty feelings about Leola which Boy often discussed with Ramsay. "As long as he loved Leola," he would argue, "these encounters with other girls didn't really count. Or did they?" Ramsay was ashamed that he didn't have the strength to tell Boy not to tell him about all this, but he was too curious not to keep listening. Actually, he was envious that Boy had Leola, and spitefully liked to hear of the difficulties the relationship was having.

As for himself, he did not try to find a girlfriend because he still thought a lot about Diana. Even though he knew he had been right to reject her, he still sometimes missed her delightful personality and her intelligent conversation.

Commentary

What Dunstan Ramsay decides to do with his life gets underway in this chapter. He prudently manages his money to ensure that he can get what he wants — a university education in history up to the M.A. level. He thinks this education should be well-rounded, including many subjects other than history, and he says that there is one special branch of history which has attracted him particularly. His future career will be based on this educational foundation.

He is still a loner, without any close friends or even a girlfriend. At this stage of life — one in which he knows he is not "blossoming" — he is sensibly and intelligently working hard to prepare for his future.

Davies allows us to see how unusual Ramsay is in his pursuits by comparing him to Boy Staunton. Boy is much more typical of the young people of the 1920s than Ramsay. In fact, he seems like "the quintessence of the Jazz age, a Scott Fitzgerald character." F. Scott Fitzgerald, a writer, had portrayed people much like Boy in novels such as *The Great Gatsby* during the 1920s. Youth and energy were greatly valued since they were well-suited for a life of drinking (illegal because Prohibition was in effect) and wild parties. Even Boy's name suggests this youthfulness, as do his fashionable clothes. Boy is able to keep up a high style of living because he is rich. His wealth is not simply inherited from his father, but is also the result of his own shrewd business sense. He is attending law school to prepare either for business or politics; he has encouraged his father to expand his sugar beet interests to include buying into the industries that will refine the sugar beets into sugar; and he has made some good investments in the stock market.

Davies sums up the difference between the two men when Ramsay says, "to him the reality of life lay in external things, whereas for me the only reality was of the spirit — of the mind." However, Ramsay is not so unworldly that he does not take advantage of Boy's business sense to make some money for himself. Nor is he free of jealousy and spite, for he perversely enjoys Boy's confessions about his problems with Leola. Ramsay is right in saying "youth was not my time to flower."

CHAPTER 2

Summary

Ramsay completed his university education and became a schoolmaster at Colborne College. He chose a boys' school because he didn't want to teach girls, believing that they should have a different kind of education than boys. He could also avoid spending another year getting a teaching certificate by teaching at a private school.

Ramsay believed he was a good teacher. He insisted on high standards, didn't have favourites, never tried to be popular and knew his subject well. As he became more interested in the relationship between history and myth, he taught more and more about it. As time went by, it became clear that he was not a homosexual, a "suspicion that hangs over every bachelor schoolmaster." In fact, he quite disliked boys. He never thought that he would stay there for forty years.

Teaching was his professional life in which he did his duty well, but he also had a larger life that had its inspiration from other sources. It is about this larger life that he wants to convey to the Headmaster in this memoir, so that when he is dead, one man at least will know the truth about him and come to his defence.

Although Ramsay was critical of Boy's sexual escapades, he did not live a chaste life. While he was a schoolmaster, he became intimately involved with a number of women whom he had no intention of marrying. But he never treated women merely as objects.

His affairs with women were usually brief because his sense of humour put them off. So did his preference for talking a lot while making love. Furthermore, his physical disabilities interfered. It would be many years before he discovered real love again.

Commentary

This section is full of clever allusions which Davies uses for comic effect. In describing the women he has known while at Colborne College, Ramsay refers to Agnes Day, Gloria Mundy and Libby Doe. The first two of these names are allusions to Latin terms used in the Anglican church service. Agnes Day suggests *agnus dei*, which means "lamb of God," or Christ in his role as sacrificial victim. This name suits Agnes, who "yearned to take upon herself the sins of the whole world, and sacrifice her body and mind to some deserving male's cause." The name Gloria Mundy suggests the Latin phrase *gloria mundi*, which means "the glories of the world." Suitably enough, Gloria is "a good-time girl, who has to be stoked with costly food, theater tickets, and joy rides of all kinds." Finally, the name Libby Doe, is an allusion to a Latin term used by Freud in his psychoanalytic theory. *Libido* is the sexual or pleasure-seeking aspect of the personality. Libby, true to the implications of her name, "thought sex was the one great, true, and apostolic key and cure and could not get enough."

CHAPTER 3

Summary

At 26, Ramsay obtained his M.A., and his $5000, invested with Boy's advice, had become $8000. Boy had made an unknown but large amount of money. Boy married Leola in the Presbyterian Church in Deptford. Ramsay was their best man. Leola was a radiant bride. Her parents, who were overshadowed by the Stauntons, wept with joy. Some others, however, grinned.

It was the most fashionable wedding ever in Deptford, even though some of Boy's law school friends got drunk at the Tecumseh House after the teetotaller reception at the Staunton's. Although Doc Staunton was very rich, Ramsay could see that Boy would become even richer.

Ramsay ended up, by chance, on the same ship to Europe — the *Melita* — as the one Boy and Leola took on their honeymoon. Ramsay had decided to treat himself to a holiday. But whereas Boy and Leola were traveling first class on the upper deck, Ramsay was a second class passenger below. Boy came to see Ramsay three or four times during the trip; Leola only waved to him once during the ship's concert.

Boy met everyone in first class, but was most impressed with the Reverend George Maldon Leadbeater. He was from a fashionable New York church and his unusual religious views were attractive to Boy.

According to Leadbeater, Christ was a social and economic success. At the marriage at Cana, in his opinion, Christ "helped the host out of a tight place when the drinks gave out, because He had probably been in the same fix Himself in His days in business and knew what social embarrassment was."

Boy was also impressed that Leadbeater appreciated beauty and dressed well. He even carried around a handful of semi-precious gems in his pocket which he took out two or three times a day just to look at.

Ramsay never met Leadbeater because Boy claimed he couldn't take Ramsay up to first class, and also said that he wouldn't want to ask Leadbeater to come down to second class. But Ramsay doubted the sincerity of Leadbeater. He also saw that Leadbeater's idea of the beautiful was nothing more than sickly sentimentality.

Commentary

Davies uses the setting on board ship symbolically. Boy, Leola and the Reverend Leadbeater are all on the upper deck, traveling first class, while Ramsay is below, in second class. This physical division suggests the "classes" of society to which these characters belong. Because of their economic success, those on the upper deck are "higher" on the social scale. Because Ramsay is not as rich, he is "lower" on the scale. Although Boy "comes down" to visit Ramsay, he makes it clear that Ramsay should not expect people from "first class" to mix with people from "second class."

This symbolic setting is ironic. Davies does not really think that the first class passengers are better than the second class passengers. In fact, he thinks just the opposite. He disapproves of the rating of people by material values alone. Because Leadbeater makes more money than any minister in Deptford, it does not mean he is a better man. This irony is most clearly shown in Leadbeater's distorted interpretation of Christianity. By turning Christ into a successful businessman, he misses the whole spiritual dimension of Christianity. As the Bible says, "blessed are the poor, for they shall inherit the kingdom of heaven."

CHAPTER 4

Summary

When the ship docked in Southampton, England, Boy and Leola got off. Ramsay continued to Antwerp, Belgium, because he wanted to go back and look at the battlefields where he had fought during the war. Now they looked very different. They were all tidy, not muddy. He tried to find the statue of the little Madonna, but he couldn't. When he described it to people there, they couldn't help him. So Ramsay left.

Because he really wanted to track that statue down, he became interested in medieval and Renaissance art, especially religious art. He began to study Madonnas of every period. Soon, he knew enough to be able to describe accurately the one he was trying to find: it was "a Virgin of the Immaculate Conception, of polychromed wood, about twenty-four inches high, and most probably of Flemish or North German workmanship of the period between 1675 and 1725."

Ramsay spent the rest of the summer looking through many churches in the Low Countries, France, Austria and Italy. Not only was he finding out about religious art, he was also learning about religion. He concentrated on the saints. The interest in detail that had once made him want to be a polymath was now useful in acquiring information about the saints. He could learn easily about St. Anthony and his bell, St. Sebastian full of arrows and St. Roche with the dog and a bad leg. He became conceited about the wide extent of his knowledge about saints, and started trying to find saints that were rare so he could add them to his vast knowledge. He needed to learn German to find out more, so he decided to study it the next winter. He was confident he could learn anything he needed to help in his work.

It didn't occur to him that these saints were probably once real people who had done something unusual during their lives. Studying the saints deepened his religious sense and made him think what he had sensed as a child, that religion and *Arabian Nights* were close in spirit. He had found a career that he knew would bring him lasting happiness.

Commentary

Ramsay's trip overseas widens his horizon still further. In pursuing the study of saints as a means to finding the statue of the little Madonna he had seen on the battlefield in France, he finds an interest in life which makes him deeply happy. His happiness is closely related to the deepening of his religious sense which occurs as he thinks about the saints.

CHAPTER 5

Summary

Back at Colborne College, Ramsay continued his teaching duties. He developed a professional attitude towards the chore of marking the boys' homework, which helped him to do it cheerfully. Unlike the other teachers, he did not have to supervise sports because of his artificial leg.

Ramsay liked teaching at the college. He knew his boys and knew his work, so his students did well on exams. He also liked most of his colleagues. He thought private schools had an advantage over public schools because they allowed eccentrics to teach in them.

Boy was also doing some teaching. He was training Leola to become the kind of wife he thought he needed: a well-mannered and well-dressed woman who could play bridge and tennis and make light conversation with his business friends. He was controlling her life in every way, deciding, for example, that she should not have any children until he was fully established in the sugar business. She adored him and did everything he wanted.

Boy was a genius at making money. He would borrow money he didn't need, then repay it before the interest came due. Then he would borrow a larger amount in the same way. Soon he established good credit for large sums with the bank, and was respected at the head office.

In 1927 something happened that made him even more successful. The Prince of Wales came to Canada to make a tour, and Boy was selected to be one of his aides-de-camp. Boy went with the Prince when he paid a visit to Colborne College and travelled across Canada, accompanying him on his tour. Leola showed up from time to time on the tour because she loved Boy so much she wanted to please him. Ramsay had never seen a woman more in love with a man than Leola. He was happy for her and wished her well.

After the Prince had gone, Boy and Leola settled down and began a family. Their first child was named Edward David after the Prince, who sent a christening mug with the royal motto *Ich dien* (I serve) on it.

Commentary

As in Chapter 1 of Part Three, Ramsay contrasts his lifestyle with that of Boy. While Boy moves on to greater wealth and higher social prestige, Ramsay leads a relatively humdrum life as a teacher.

Davies' style, however, allows the reader to see indirectly how critical he is of the way Boy is conducting his life, no matter how successful it may appear on the surface. Davies describes his rise to new heights in a tongue-in-cheek way which reveals his opinion. By comparing Boy's materialistic success to the rise of a "cherub" into "the heaven of finance," for example, or as one who is moving up through the ranks from "cherub" to "angel" and then to "archangel," Davies highlights the absence of spiritual values in Boy's life. In describing Boy and Leola's settling down, he says they did so "in a modest manner" when he means quite the opposite. In pointing out that they were "serious, responsible Young Marrieds" he intends us to see that they are neither serious nor responsible. Asking "how *could* H.R.H. have known?" about the birth of Staunton's son, he implies that Boy has taken advantage of his role as aide-de-camp to the Prince to tell him he has named a son after him, in the hope that the Prince will in some way acknowledge the event.

CHAPTER 6

Summary

Boy Staunton's parents never visited Boy and Leola because they disapproved of drinking and because Boy and Leola had left the Presbyterian Church to become Anglicans. In 1924, the rich Presbyterians and the poor Methodists had joined to form the United Church, a union which led to many jokes. Some people, objecting to the new United Church, had become Anglicans. It was impossible at that time not to belong to a church officially, for the census-taker insisted that everyone state their religious denomination. Boy and Leola had joined a fashionable Anglican church which did not demand that they become confirmed. However, they did have their son, David, confirmed and also their daughter, Caroline, who was born two years later.

Boy objected to Ramsay's references to his study of saints, and this made Ramsay all the more determined to make such references. Boy thought that saints were for Catholics and ignorant people. Meanwhile, Boy advised Ramsay to stop being a schoolmaster: "If you don't hurry up and let life know what you want, life will damned soon show you what you'll get," he said to Ramsay. But Ramsay was not sure he wanted to give orders to life. He preferred to let life take its course. In 1928, events took an unexpected turn which were to greatly affect his life.

The Headmaster at the time — who was two Headmasters before the one to whom Ramsay is writing — used to bring in outside speakers to the school. One day he invited Mr. Joel Surgeoner, who was the head of the Lifeline Mission in Toronto which helped people who were down and out. Surgeoner was not well educated and seemed sincere, although Ramsay suspected him of being a liar.

Surgeoner spoke about how he ran the Mission by begging. Sometimes, when they needed something badly, like blankets, he would pray and they would just appear. Ramsay didn't believe this. Suddenly, Surgeoner turned on him and accused Ramsay of disbelief. He said that if Ramsay went down to the Mission he could see for himself. Everyone scowled at Ramsay and applauded Surgeoner. Ironically, Ramsay recognized him when he turned around as none other than the tramp who had been caught with Mrs. Dempster in Deptford.

That night, Ramsay did go down to the Mission where a service was in progress. Surgeoner was praying for the things they currently needed there. Ramsay observed that he wore a hearing aid. Surgeoner nodded in recognition to him and went on to give examples of people being "saved." The meeting ended with a revival hymn about a lifeline, and Ramsay was finally alone with Surgeoner. Surgeoner showed him about fifty men lying on cots in a dormitory provided for by begging and prayer. Ramsay told him that his talk at Colborne College would bring him $543. Meanwhile, his service that evening had only brought in 13 cents. Ramsay said that that was all the service was worth. Surgeoner replied that, although the facts of his stories were not true, they were true in the spirit and gave hope to the desperate. The tricky means he used served God's ends, he believed.

Then Ramsay told him that he knew who he was. Surgeoner replied that his experience with Mrs. Dempster had turned him to God. He described how awful it was to be a tramp. Tramps, he said, were madmen, criminals and degenerates. Starving and living outside make men savages. He had become a tramp after a quarrel with his father, and he took to drink: shoe-blacking, fermented prunes, or sugar beets provided the alcohol. He explained that the sex life of tramps is brutal. Mostly, it consisted of sodomy. In fact, that's how he lost his hearing: a gang of older tramps raped him and beat him up. That night in Deptford he had refused a meal of rabbit and carrots, even though he was starving, because he would have had to submit to this kind of sex in exchange. When he met Mrs. Dempster, she had seemed like an angel to him. He had asked her for money, then attacked her when she said she had none. When she was kind to him, he began to cry, asked her for sex and she cooperated. The encounter seemed like "glory coming into my life," Surgeoner said. It was a cleansing and purifying experience. He ran out of the town like a man cleansed of devils. "She was a blessed saint," he told Ramsay. "It was a miracle."

Ramsay had put Mrs. Dempster and Deptford right out of his mind, but now he realized he must go back and include all that in his life again. He gave Surgeoner ten dollars which would be used for the things they needed.

Commentary

This chapter contains two philosophical concepts that are

important to the development of Dunstan Ramsay's life. First, unlike Boy Staunton, who sets out to control every aspect of life, Ramsay commits himself to "the Greek notion of allowing Chance to take a formative hand in my affairs." If he had not adopted this attitude to life, he would not have been led into a situation with Surgeoner which resulted in changing his life plan.

That change in life plan forms the second philosophical concept in the chapter. Up to this point, Ramsay has thought that it is best to put Deptford and Mrs. Dempster firmly into the past. If he were a character like Boy Staunton, nothing would change his mind. But Ramsay, after hearing Surgeoner's story about the "miracle" Mrs. Dempster performed for him, decides that "there was to be no release by muffling up the past." He knew that "any new life must include Deptford." Ramsay's thoughtful flexibility (the opposite of Boy's determined drive to success) will have unforeseen good results.

CHAPTER 7

Summary

Ramsay went back to Deptford and obtained the address of the aunt who had taken in Mrs. Dempster. She was a spinster named Miss Bertha Shanklin who lived in Weston. Ramsay got the address from the magistrate whom he visited on the pretense of finding out what to do about the man who still owed him money for the *Banner*.

The magistrate asked Ramsay if he knew who had thrown the snowball that caused all the trouble. He said there was guilt somewhere. He had never seen such grief as Mrs. Dempster's when she realized that Paul had run away. She had needed injections of morphia before Miss Shanklin could take her away. Ramsay wanted to see the whole incident as an accident, but he realized that the magistrate thought he really did know something. Ramsay said nothing.

However, Ramsay felt guilty all over again and wanted to talk to someone about it, so he went to see the Catholic priest. This was a foolish choice. Ramsay thought Mrs. Dempster should be declared a saint, but the Catholic priest didn't agree. He thought that reforming a tramp and appearing on the battlefield as a Madonna were hardly actions worthy of saint-hood. As for raising Willie from the dead, he believed Dr.

McCausland's version of the story, that Willie never really was dead. The priest told Ramsay that only the Catholic church had the right to declare someone a saint, and pointed out that he and Mrs. Dempster were not Catholics. Therefore, he advised him to forget the whole business. He added that when he was studying to be a priest, he was warned about a creature called a "fool-saint." This was a Jewish idea that there are people who do a great deal of good, but it all comes to nothing because they are fools. He suggested that Mrs. Dempster was a "fool-saint" and not a real saint.

Ramsay hated the priest for telling him this, and within a week he was at Weston talking with his fool-saint, Mrs. Dempster.

Commentary

This chapter demonstrates once again the inadequacy of conventional religion in dealing with the kind of spirituality Ramsay is pursuing. He turns to the Roman Catholic priest to discuss Mrs. Dempster, thinking that of all the formal religions, Roman Catholicism will be the most likely to understand and sympathize with what he sees as her tremendous significance. On the contrary, however, the Catholic priest is not open to consider anything other than the strict dogma he has been taught. He immediately rejects the possibility that Mrs. Dempster may be a saint, and neatly fits her, instead, into a category that enables him to continue his low opinion of her. She is to him a "fool-saint," an important concept since it forms the title for Part Three of the novel. Looked at conventionally, Mrs. Dempster is an example of "virtue tainted with madness," in other words a fool-saint. But Ramsay continues to sense that she really may be a genuine saint, capable of miracles.

CHAPTER 8

Summary

Mrs. Dempster was now 40, but she looked younger. Her expression was sweet and her dress simple, probably homemade by the aunt. She couldn't remember Ramsay, but when he talked about Paul, she became upset and the aunt took her out of the room.

Mrs. Shanklin was small and had a gentle manner. Her house was pretty in an old-fashioned and genteel way. Ramsay arrived without warning her because he rightly guessed that she would not want him to see her niece. She explained after ten minutes that Ramsay should leave because talking about the past always upset Mrs. Dempster. Ramsay tried to soften her up by talking about how kind Mrs. Dempster had been to him as a child, how his mother had helped her and about his guilt at not coming to see her before this. He did not mention saints.

Miss Shanklin explained what had happened to Mrs. Dempster before she came to Deptford. How Amasa had resented the fact that there was a little money in the family and how Miss Shanklin had been too proud to help them at the time they got married. Now she regretted acting that way and confessed to Ramsay that, although she had never seen Paul, she wished that she had had an opportunity to help him. She loved her niece very much because she was all the family she had left. Then Miss Shanklin cried a bit and went to ask the hired girl for some tea. Soon she and Ramsay were on good terms. She appreciated hearing from him how good and sweet Mrs. Dempster was, even after her terrible accident. She asked him if it really was an accident that had injured her. She said that Mary had been full of hope before marrying Amasa.

Miss Shanklin admitted she felt guilty about her niece because she had missed the opportunity to help her. Now she thought it best not to recall the painful past with her because she always thought of Paul and cried. She invited Ramsay to come again to see Mrs. Dempster if he promised not to mention the past. She also told Ramsay that Mrs. Dempster remembered Amasa only as "a blue mouth, like a rotten hole . . . telling God he forgave her for ruining his life." She added that Amasa had died praying.

Commentary

For once, Ramsay's craftiness is turned to a constructive purpose. Probably from years of practice dealing with his mother, he is able to sense the best means of getting around Miss Shanklin so that he can see Mrs. Dempster and keep coming to visit her in the future. He cleverly arrives at her door without warning because he correctly thinks she would probably not allow him to see Mrs. Dempster. He carefully observes her personality and the nature of her house and rightly concludes that this is not a person to whom he should mention his real purpose for coming — his study of the saints. Instead, he cleverly flatters her niece, telling Miss Shanklin all the good things about her that he can think of and making sure that she realizes that his mother had given Mrs. Dempster a great deal of help. But it is his admission of his guilt about Mrs. Dempster which has the most effect on Miss Shanklin. Even here, however, he is not completely truthful about the reasons for his guilt. He only says that he feels guilty that he has not tried to see her before this. When Miss Shanklin asks about the so-called "accident" which has made Mary the way she is, he keeps quiet, though this is what he actually feels guilty about.

Miss Shanklin is in the right state to hear about his guilt, because she herself feels guilty about her niece. Her guilt stems from the time when the Dempsters got married. At that time, Miss Shanklin could have helped out, but was too proud and too critical of the way Amasa and Mary married to bother with them. Now that events have turned out so badly for her niece, she wishes she had helped earlier on in their marriage. Ramsay craftily manipulates the conversation in such a way that he strikes a common feeling — that of guilt — with Miss Shanklin. By this means, he gets his own way.

CHAPTER 9

Summary

In May, 1929, Boy called Ramsay to tell him to sell some of his stocks. When the stock market crashed, Ramsay was not ruined financially as were most of his colleagues at the school.

Ramsay was not concentrating on his financial affairs. He was eagerly waiting for the end of term so he could go back to Europe and continue his study of the saints. Every summer from then on, except during the 1939-45 war, he went overseas. As a result of these trips, he published his book, *A Hundred Saints for Travellers*, which was still selling well in six languages, and also nine other books and some articles. On this particular trip he was looking for information about a saint usually called Wilgefortis, but also referred to by many other names.

Wilgefortis was a saint supposed to intercede for girls who had suitors they didn't like. She originated in Portugal. She was said to have miraculously grown a heavy beard when she prayed for help to avoid marriage. Her suitor, the King of Sicily, rejected her and her angry father crucified her. Ramsay tracked down every shrine of this odd saint and compared all the many versions of the legend. In England, where she was known as Uncumber, there had once been a shrine for her in St. Paul's.

Ramsay wanted to test two ideas he had of Uncumber. He thought she might be an example of the hermaphrodite figure of the Great Mother worshipped in Cyprus and Carthage. She might also be an example of a phenomenon recently discussed by two New York doctors: that unusually emotional women sometimes grew abnormal amounts of hair, especially facial hair.

Ramsay's travels took him through France to Austria where he stayed in a Tyrolean village. There he came across a circus called *Le grand Cirque forain de St. Vite*. He saw that the circus featured a bearded lady and went to see the show. After seeing some acrobats, the Human Frog, the Wild Man, a dwarf who danced on dull, broken glass, a man with a lump on his chest that looked like an imperfect twin and the Bearded Lady, Ramsay was about to leave. Then who should appear on the stage but Paul Dempster to perform some card tricks. His tricks were so well-performed that they were too good for the audience. He elegantly and deftly did some of the tricks Ramsay had taught him long ago. He spoke in French and sometimes in German.

After the performance, Ramsay went over to him and spoke in English; Paul replied in French. When Ramsay switched into French, he changed to German. In the end, he admitted that he was Paul Dempster, but he had used the name Faustus Legrand for more years than the ten he had been known as Paul Dempster. When Ramsay mentioned his mother, he did not answer.

Little by little, Ramsay got on better terms with him. It helped warm things up when he offered to buy drinks for the whole circus troupe. Ramsay did his best to become popular with this group by talking to them about themselves. All these freakish people talked freely to him because they were off-duty and wanted to be regarded simply as ordinary people. Ramsay talked about Uncumber to the Bearded Lady, who was very interested. In fact, they all thought Ramsay's search for information about saints was so odd that he was a kind of freak himself.

Ramsay judged that the others might talk to him about Paul, so he got Paul out of the way by sending him for more liquor. They explained to him that Paul stayed with the troupe because he felt loyal to Le Solitaire who had helped him get started with the circus.

It was a merry party. Ramsay danced with the Bearded Lady to music whistled by the dwarf. They all laughed to see a one-legged man dance. He had a short talk with Paul before leaving. Paul said he had no interest in his mother anymore. He blamed himself for her condition because he had always been told that it was his birth that had caused her madness. He thought she would be better off dead.

The next morning, Ramsay set off to find out more about Uncumber. But first he had to get more money at the bank. Someone — Paul, he thought — had stolen his wallet at the circus.

Commentary

This chapter documents Ramsay's "blossoming" as a scholar of saints. In his quest to find out about Uncumber, all his talents for detailed observation and clever interviewing become useful. In his accidental meeting with Paul Dempster in Tyrol can be seen the widening range of his new life. It is a great adventure for Ramsay, and he finds a direct outlet for his discoveries by writing books that are to become extremely popular and useful.

Ironically, Paul himself has felt just as guilty about the condition of his mother as Ramsay has. Indeed, it now becomes clear that at least three people blame themselves for her suffering: Ramsay, Paul and Miss Shanklin. Only Boy, who actually threw the snowball, as yet feels no guilt.

PART FOUR • CHAPTER 1

Summary
Boy made a lot of money in the Depression because of a particular theory; people without much money wanted sweet food and drink to cheer themselves and feel full. His sugar companies did a good business under his controlling company called Alpha Corporation.

He branched out to acquire a large bread company. He promised the price would not go up, but he made money by reducing the quality of the loaves. He refused to start a beer company because he didn't want to upset his father who had become a larger holder in Alpha.

Boy became so rich that his wealth could only be estimated. Politicians complained of the imbalance in wealth: while Boy had millions, many people were nearly starving. But these politicians continued to buy his sugar products. Ramsay's colleagues at the school denounced Boy as a "ca-*pittle*-ist" (as the word capitalist used to be pronounced then). Ramsay never admitted that he knew Boy personally.

His friendship with Boy continued because Boy needed someone whom he could confide in about his troubles with Leola. She could not keep up with Boy's genius for making money. He continued to use his slight friendship with the Prince of Wales to advance his career.

Boy and Ramsay were both 32, but Boy looked younger. Leola was a little younger, but she was starting to show her age. She still insisted on being girlish and buying frilly clothes that were not fashionable. She had never really learned to speak in the cultivated and sophisticated way Boy wanted. Early in the marriage, she had rebelled against Boy's attempts to "educate" her, but now she gave in and tried to be what he wanted.

For Boy it was easy to acquire better manners and speech. He was learning all the time without much effort. So, after six years of marriage, Boy had changed a lot but Leola hadn't. Looking back, Ramsay could see that there was a continuous tension between them. He didn't want to be the peacemaker in their fights. He preferred to be the "Friend of the Family." He now only felt pity for Leola because she was unable to live up to Boy's image of her.

There were two occasions when Ramsay did get involved in their fights. One time, in 1926, Boy asked him to teach Leola the philosophy of Dr. Emile Coué. Boy thought she would improve by means of the auto-suggestion Coué taught. But Leola was unable to turn herself into the kind of woman Boy wanted by this method. Ramsay told Boy that it was possible to try too hard to accomplish something, but Boy disagreed. He argued that he had become better and better by his own willpower, and Leola should do the same.

The second time Ramsay came between Boy and Leola was more serious. It was late in 1927, after the Royal Tour. Boy asked him to develop some rolls of film which contained many pictures of Leola naked in suggestive poses. Ramsay was angry and confused about Boy's motives, but he returned the pictures without saying anything and waited to see what would happen.

Next time he went to dinner there, Boy brought out the pictures in front of Leola who wanted to leave the room in embarrassment. But Boy forced her to stay while they discussed the photos. Boy enjoyed Ramsay's discomfort and tried to get him to admit it. But Ramsay claimed that the situation was not so unusual after all. It was just like the situation in an old legend about Gyges and King Candaules. This king was so proud of his wife's beauty that he insisted his friend Gyges should see her naked. Ramsay pointed out that there were two versions of the end of the story. In one, the Queen and Gyges fall in love and force the king off his throne. In the other, Gyges kills King Candaules. Boy discounted both endings as being impossible for Ramsay.

Ramsay thought Boy was excited by the evening's events, for by his calculation that was the very night on which their son was conceived.

Commentary

Once more, the character of Ramsay is developed by contrast with Boy Staunton. On the surface, Boy seems to be a tremendous success. His economic and social status continue to increase in scope and power. But Ramsay is able to see beneath the surface. He sees that Boy is not happy, despite his success. His unhappiness is largely due to his shaky marriage. Now Ramsay sees that the quarrels between Leola and Boy "were sharp outbreaks in a continuous campaign." Leola has gone as far as she can with only a pretty face to recommend her. Boy has developed an impossibly high standard for her because he treats her like an object: "his idea of a wife for himself would have had the beauty and demeanour of Lady Diana Manners coupled with the wit of Margot Asquith.''

The steely determination that has made Boy a "genius" in business, also makes him a poor husband. He cannot see that a woman is not an object to be "polished" into something perfect. Therefore, he is incapable of seeing Leola as a person with needs of her own.

Both episodes in which Ramsay becomes involved in their quarrels are examples of Boy's egotistic will. In the first, Ramsay tries to tell him not to force Leola to do anything. It is possible to try too hard. In the second, where Boy captures Leola in photos that show her the way he wants to see her (as a pretty sex object), he enrages Ramsay by tantalizing him with what he has lost.

In this way, Boy builds up his own ego and uses Ramsay's discomfort to feed his own sexual excitement. Compared to previous chapters that show Ramsay's happiness in pursuit of his saints, Boy emerges as a spiritually impoverished man.

CHAPTER 2

Summary

Every fortnight Ramsay took the train to see Mrs. Dempster at Miss Shanklin's. He only stayed for lunch each time because his visits were tiring to Mrs. Dempster. He did as he had agreed and did not mention the past. He was pleased to see that Mrs. Dempster was kept clean and neat by her aunt.

The only other man Ramsay ever met there was Miss Shanklin's lawyer, Orpheus Wettenhall, a small, laughing man with a big walrus moustache and silver-rimmed glasses. He was fond of hunting and invited Ramsay to come with him, but Ramsay refused, saying that he could not hunt with his bad leg.

In February 1932, Miss Shanklin got pneumonia and died. Wettenhall wrote to tell Ramsay and invited him to the funeral. After the funeral, he told Ramsay that Miss Shanklin had named him executor of her estate on one condition: he would inherit $5000 a year if he would agree to take care of Mrs. Dempster. This offer made Ramsay happy. It was a chance for him to do something positive for Mrs. Dempster, and he began to feel less guilty about her. In addition, this new position would give him the opportunity to observe her closely and see whether she really was a saint or not. He thought studying her might result in a book on the psychology of religion.

Two days later, he was told that Orpheus Wettenhall had shot himself. The police explained to him that Wettenhall had been using the money of all his clients, Miss Shanklin included, for investments. The stock market crash of 1929 had wiped out a lot of this money, and he had used up Miss Shanklin's income to keep himself solvent. Her death meant that this information would have to come to light and he couldn't bear the shame, so he committed suicide. The police wished to keep this information secret. Although it did leak out, they tried to cover it up by saying publicly he had a hunting accident.

Even though there were other old people whose money he had spent who would now be destitute, people had liked Wettenhall and felt sorry for him. People almost blamed Miss Shanklin for dying too soon. Ramsay concluded that popularity and good character are unrelated, and also that pity makes people stop thinking realistically.

So Miss Shanklin's inheritance was reduced to only $221. The only way Ramsay could support Mrs. Dempster was to pay her expenses himself, which he decided to do. This was especially difficult because Colborne College was not doing well financially, and all the schoolmasters there, including Ramsay, had agreed to take a cut in salary. The best Ramsay could do for her was to place her in a public hospital for the insane in Toronto where he could see her often.

He felt badly taking her there. There wasn't enough staff and the place was old, dark and smelly. When he left her there, Mrs. Dempster looked as unhappy as she had been during her worst days in Deptford. Ramsay felt mean, but he had no other choice.

Commentary

As Ramsay continues to mature, he develops high moral principles. He observes what happens in life and considers the right and wrong of what he sees.

In the events that lead up to his taking charge of Mrs. Dempster, he has much to consider from a moral point of view. He is shocked to see the way people react to the suicide of Orpheus Wettenhall. Because Orpheus is a pleasant man popular with the people of Weston, everyone overlooks the real wrong he has done. He has, in fact, embezzled money from his clients, first to invest illegally in the stock market, and then to pay for his own expenses after the stock market crashes. Most of his clients, like Miss Bertha Shanklin, are old people who have trusted him to manage their money. Furthermore, they really need this money. But Orpheus is so popular that people feel sorry for his death instead of seeing that his dilemma is very much his own fault.

Unlike the inhabitants of Weston, Ramsay does not feel sorry for Wettenhall. He feels sorrier for the old men and women whom Wettenhall has tricked. Ramsay, therefore, is being sarcastic when he says of these real victims: "Nobody had time or pity for these minor characters in the drama; all public compassion was for Orph Wettenhall." Ramsay's high moral principles are thus compared to public opinion which does not assess the situation clearly, but is sentimental and emotional instead.

CHAPTER 3

Summary

This was the most demanding time of Ramsay's life because he got involved with the Bollandists and pursued his study of the saints with great delight.

The Bollandists were a group of Jesuits who were dedicated to recording all available information about saints in their *Acta Sanctorum*. They were named after John van Bolland who began this work in 1643. In 1837, they began publishing the series beginning with the saints' days in January. After 69 volumes, they had catalogued all the saints up to those in November. They also published a yearly collection of additional material about saints called the *Analecta Bollandiana*.

Ramsay found it interesting to see who got to be saints in any given period. He concluded that saints tended to reflect the age which produced them, and that the selection of saints was actually a political process. He couldn't afford the *Acta*, but he did buy a second-hand run of the *Analecta*. His students were impressed that he could read in French, German and Latin. His colleagues thought he was an eccentric and even worried that he might be turning into a Roman Catholic. In 1932, he was busy learning medieval Greek so that he could read more articles in that language.

One day he had the idea of sending his own notes on

Uncumber to the editor of *Acta*, Hippolyte Delehaye. He received a letter back asking his permission to print the notes in the *Analecta* and inviting him to come and see them if he were ever in Brussels. Ramsay was delighted. He even boasted about it to his colleagues who were indifferent. He also told Boy, who didn't really understand, but who did grasp the fact that Ramsay was becoming an important scholar in his field. Boy began inviting Ramsay to larger parties to show him off to his business friends.

This gave Ramsay more opportunity to observe Boy and his friends. He found them strange, and would not have changed places with them, even though they were rich. They talked a lot about "politics," but unintelligently. They spoke about "the ordinary fellow" and claimed "he" could not think straight and wanted to get the rewards for things "he" had not helped to make. They thought every man could be rich like themselves if he could overcome these two faults. But Ramsay saw that they were rich because they had a special talent for manipulating money which ordinary people did not have. Listening to the ideas of these men, Ramsay thought he must be the only person in the world without a plan that promised to resolve every problem.

At first, he thought he might fit in with the Bollandists. He spent several happy weeks in Brussels because the Bollandists treated him well as a special friend. But sometimes he doubted his own choices in life. He would ask himself why, at 34, he still had no wife and children, why he thought teaching was important and why he continued to pursue such an odd subject as the history of saints. He even considered going to Harvard for a Ph.D. so that he could take a job in a university.

But then he would turn again eagerly to his studies. He decided to stick with his idea that any serious study would give an insight into the nature of life and the purpose of man. He would keep on, knowing from his study of what happens to saints that if a revelation did come, it would come unexpectedly.

He got to know almost all the Bollandists, even though he never lost his Protestant distrust of Catholics. Eventually, though, he knew that he would always be an outsider to them, much as they liked him. When he said goodbye to Père Delehaye, he was told that he would always be their friend and could always write and visit.

The next day he left for Vienna by train with the eccentric

Bollandist, Padre Ignacio Blazon. Blazon was a dramatic figure, unlike the other Bollandists. He wore his soutane all the time, his battered black hat looked like something out of an opera and his glasses were mended with dirty string. He had a big red nose and many missing teeth. He took snuff frequently. The other priests put up with him because he was supposed to be very old and also he was extremely learned. He could speak many languages.

Ramsay liked him and found a good way to enjoy his company. Blazon loved food, but didn't like to pay for it, so Ramsay took him out to many of the best restaurants in Brussels. There, over dinner, Blazon would loudly tell Ramsay many stories about the saints. His stories emphasized the "underworld" of saints. He described St. Joseph, for example, as a patron saint for cuckolds, since Mary had become pregnant by someone other than her husband. To Blazon, such earthy stories about the saints did not show disrespect. He thought they supplied the side of a saint's character that legend had suppressed. "Mankind," he theorized, "cannot endure perfection; it stifles him. He demands that even saints should cast a shadow." Few saints, he observed, are wise.

When they boarded the train, Blazon ensured that no one else would want to share their carriage by reading loudly from his prayer book. Ramsay brought a substantial lunch, including brandy and wine. Blazon wanted to start drinking at once. He continued to talk in a loud voice to Ramsay. He brought up the subject of Mrs. Dempster and Ramsay's desire to have her made a saint. He advised forgetting about it. After all, many things seem like miracles in life. Even Blazon's own birth once seemed like a miracle, for he was the first son in his Spanish family after seven girls.

Blazon went on to tell Ramsay all about his past. He had been committed by his mother to the priesthood before birth and had easily lived up to this expectation because he was "too good to be true." Even now, at 76, he was still a virgin, prizing his chastity. Although people kept trying to tempt him, one way or another, he eventually took his vows as a Jesuit and had done useful work for the Bollandists ever since. He admitted, however, that he had reached a kind of male menopause late in life which brought difficulties. He found that some aspects of Christian belief were hard to support. Since then he had been having a struggle to reconcile the wisdom of the body with the wisdom of the spirit.

As for Mrs. Dempster, he advised Ramsay to try to understand what role she has played in his own personal mythology. "You must find your answer in psychological truth, not in objective truth," he added. Perhaps God had used her as a means of making Ramsay a religious man. Whatever Ramsay did, Blazon warned, he must begin by forgiving himself for being a human being. Otherwise he might end up, like his saint, in a madhouse.

Commentary

This chapter is most important for its discussion of saints. Blazon is an expert on saints, and his words, therefore, are especially important. According to him, saints are not entirely "holy" or "good" at all. On the contrary, there have always been aspects of every saint that are very down-to-earth. Thomas Acquinas was fat; St. Jerome had a terrible temper; even the Virgin Mary may have been unfaithful to her husband. Using a term from Jungian psychology (the "Shadow" which means the dark side of the human personality), Davies makes it clear that even saints "cast a shadow" if one looks closely at all the evidence about them. Furthermore, saints are not likely to be "wise" either. People prefer a "spectacle" and wisdom tends to be quiet and unspectacular.

All this discussion about the nature of sainthood has direct bearing for the reader on the question of whether Mrs. Dempster should or should not be a saint. If saints are not entirely "holy" or "good" in terms of popular morality, then Mrs. Dempster's adultery with the tramp would in no way disqualify her for sainthood. On the contrary, she would fit in well with saints as Blazon describes them. Furthermore, her "simple-mindedness" would not be a drawback either. Saints, Blazon tells us, are not "wise;" instead they do spectacular things. This is certainly true of Mrs. Dempster.

Even though Blazon is reluctant to see Mrs. Dempster as a saint, his words give Ramsay hope that it would not be altogether impossible for his "saint" to join the many existing saints.

CHAPTER 4

Summary

Blazon continued to send Ramsay advice, usually by postcards which he wrote with purple ink. Ramsay, meanwhile, was troubled by Mrs. Dempster. She became disinterested in life and hinted how much she would like Ramsay to take her out of the institution. She wore a hat whenever he visited her, as if she were ready to go. He took her chocolates because he knew she liked giving them to the other patients.

Ramsay could tolerate the institution for an hour. To pass the time, he told the inmates stories, usually about saints. He could tell that no matter how much their minds might be damaged, they still had strong feelings. Sometimes he had to force himself to go. It was as though he were "visiting a part of his own soul that was condemned to live in hell."

He did not want to ask Boy for money to help Mrs. Dempster out. He knew that Boy didn't like to be reminded of Deptford. More important, he knew that if Boy got involved, he would take over Mrs. Dempster. Ramsay wanted to think of her as belonging to him. Ramsay could have skimped on his trips to Europe in order to provide more money for her, but he needed the rest and saw his pursuit of the saints as very important. But he did visit her forty Saturdays a year and at Easter, Christmas and on her birthday. When he was in Europe, he sent her many postcards. But he had no intention of centering his life on her madness.

Furthermore, his own life was much busier than before. He published his book *A Hundred Saints for Travellers* and was collecting information for another book to be called *The Saints: A Study in History and Popular Mythology*, in which he would explore why people needed saints. He knew it would be difficult, but he wanted to try. He was also writing articles for *Analecta* and for the Royal Historical Society.

Now Boy liked to have him around when he had other guests because Ramsay lent an air of culture to his gatherings. He could also be depended on to help out by filling in at the last minute or by talking to the dullest woman in the room. As for Ramsay, he kept up the friendship because he was still curious about Boy's life. Also, he liked him in spite of his affectations and pomposity. Furthermore, he knew that Boy's financial advice could make more money for him. In other words, his motives were mixed.

Ramsay was amazed at how important sex was to Boy. Although Boy thought that Freud's views were nonsense, he himself was a good example of Freudian psychology. Ramsay had read Freud, but was now more interested in the psychology of Carl Jung. Boy insisted that his son David only have masculine toys to play with. He even threw out a Highlander doll that David had become attached to at the age of six. He spoiled Caroline by treating her as his little sweetheart.

Leola was the one person on whom Boy spent none of his sexual attention. He told Ramsay that he needed more stimulation in bed than Leola could provide. To Ramsay, it seemed as if Boy's version of sex was a lot like an athletic workout. So Boy had a few mistresses in Montreal whom he visited on business trips. Ramsay also noticed that Boy formed erotic attachments to handsome young businessmen. Ramsay called this phenomenon "Corporation Homosexuality." Because he was familiar with the myth of Jove's cup-bearer, the handsome young Ganymedes, Ramsay could see that the pattern of an older man attracted to his young protégés was being repeated in Boy.

Boy's unfaithfulness dawned on Leola at Christmas in 1936. It was the year Boy's "friend," Edward, Prince of Wales, mounted the throne of England. His subsequent abdication to marry the American divorcée, Wallis Simpson, was a hard blow to Boy. He had thought that he would now know the King of England and that Edward VIII would set a new, gayer lifestyle for everyone.

So Christmas was a dark day for the Staunton family. Boy was depressed and sulking, and the children acted badly because they sensed something was wrong. Ramsay got annoyed at Boy and told him to grow up and stop fussing about the abdication. This put Boy into a terrible temper and he announced his intention to go for a walk. As he was getting ready, Leola found a note from one of his mistresses in Montreal in the pocket of his coat. She began to howl in grief. This made Boy furious, and he stormed out of the house to disappear for several days until after New Year's.

After a while, Ramsay went upstairs to see how Leola was doing. She was in bed, tidied up, wearing an expensive nightgown. She tried to get Ramsay to make love to her, but he refused to be used as her consolation. He left the house and eventually went back to the school intending to read, when he was told that there had been an emergency call from the Stauntons. When he returned the call, he was told that Leola was in some kind of trouble, requiring a doctor. He rushed over to find that she had tried, unsuccessfully and messily, to slash her wrists in the bathroom. The nurse handed him a note she had left which blamed him for not caring about her. He was furious that she would blame him and not Boy who had actually caused all the trouble.

After Boy's return, he and Leola managed to carry on without affection. Leola aged a great deal and her face now looked fat and empty. The children suffered most in the whole business. The nurse had gone into their rooms telling them that their mother had almost died. David became quieter and hated Christmas from then on. Caroline threw more temper tantrums.

Commentary

"As ye sow, so shall ye reap," goes the biblical proverb. Here, at last, Boy gets what he deserves. He has built his relationship with Leola on very shaky foundations, and now she turns on him. Davies cleverly links the rise and fall of Boy Staunton to the rise and fall of the Prince of Wales. At Boy's highest point of financial success, his career parallels the popular young Prince's. Now, at the very point that the Prince falls upon hard times and social humiliation, the same thing happens to Boy. Both of them have been egotistical and self-centered — a philosophy of life which Davies shows is unlikely to bring lasting satisfaction.

In contrast, Ramsay is now "blossoming" in middle age, as he did not in youth, and finds in his scholarly work a kind of delight Boy will never know.

PART FIVE • CHAPTER 1

Summary

Ramsay reports briefly on what happened during the Second World War, mainly because of events in Boy Staunton's life during that period. The war provided the opportunity for Boy to develop his industrial empire even further. He was appointed Minister of Food and proved good at the job. His Alpha Corporation and the other smaller corporations it controlled took over all aspects of food production and even developed new techniques for making concentrated, vitamin-enriched foods.

Because he spent most of his time in Ottawa doing this job, he saw little of Leola and his two children. Ramsay saw him sometimes because Boy was now a member of the school's Board of Governors. Boy's son, David, was a boarder at Colborne College, even though he could have lived at home. But Boy wanted him to be manly, and thought that being constantly in the presence of male students and teachers would accomplish this. So, from the age of ten to 18, David was at school where Ramsay often saw him.

When Leola died of pneumonia in 1942, Ramsay took David aside to tell him. Boy was overseas in England on some work connected with the Ministry and said he could not return. He asked Ramsay to look after everything that needed to be done in connection with Leola's death. Before dying, Leola had become a quiet and dull woman whose only pastime was knitting things for the Red Cross. She neglected her home and no longer did any of the things Boy had earlier tried to make her do. Ramsay could see that she was deeply unhappy, and even wondered if she had hastened her death by opening the windows after the nurse had closed them. Certainly, it was this that gave her the chill that led to her death.

David said that his mother was better off dead. Ramsay looked after him, giving up his tiny bedroom and study at the school to David during the day and arranging for him to sleep in the infirmary at night until he got over the shock. Caroline, on the other hand, made a big fuss about her mother's death, something Ramsay could not deal with. He left her in the hands of a capable schoolmistress.

Ramsay kept David with him at the funeral which was a dreary occasion one wet, late autumn day. Few people attended, though Boy's friends sent expensive flowers. Milo Papple was there, which made Ramsay remember that Milo's father had died 12 years ago. It also made him think of the Kaiser (whom Milo's father had impersonated at Ramsay's homecoming) and made him see how unfair it was that the Kaiser had lived so long. He knew he should have been thinking about Leola, but he realized that ever since he had refused to offer her comfort the Christmas Boy walked out, his relationship to her had simply been one of duty.

To Milo, the situation appeared differently. He saw Leola's death as the end of a great love affair. He also thought Ramsay must be sad because he lost Leola to Boy and then never married. But Ramsay was not sad. What he found difficult was not Leola's death, but dealing with David. David at this time seemed to Ramsay to deal in a very responsible way with events. Because Ramsay had been temporary Headmaster of the school after the official Headmaster was accidentally killed at an army training camp, he was able to see David almost every day.

In 1947, however, Boy (who had been awarded the C.B.E. for his "service" in the war) spoke to him about his future at the school. Ramsay would have been glad to stay on as Headmaster in peacetime conditions because then he would have received a much better salary and other benefits that had been impossible during the war. Boy, however, and other members of the school's Board of Governors had decided that he must be replaced. At first, Boy argued that Ramsay was too old. But Ramsay knew that was a lie. Like Boy, he was not quite fifty. Then Boy said it was because he had no wife, but Ramsay knew that also was not the real reason they wanted him out. The truth eventually came out.

To others like Boy, Ramsay seemed queer, not queer in the sense of homosexual, but queer in the sense of strange or funny. It was not that Ramsay was not a good teacher, Boy explained. It was the fact that he wanted to study the saints. That made him seem eccentric, and Boy feared that parents wouldn't want their sons to go to Colborne if he were Headmaster. Ramsay suspected that Boy already had someone else in mind for the job. Indeed he did. He named the present Headmaster (the one to whom Ramsay is addressing his whole life story) as the one for the job. So Ramsay was made chief of History and Assistant Head. He insisted that Boy make a public explanation, which would be a lie, that Ramsay wanted to step down from the job to do more research. He also demanded six months' leave with full pay. Off he would go to visit the great shrines of Latin America, starting with the Shrine of the Virgin of Guadalupe in Mexico.

Commentary

This chapter is extremely critical of Boy Staunton. Davies, however, does not criticize Boy directly, saying, for example, "Boy was dreadful because of such-and-such." Instead, he uses the technique of understatement and lets the facts speak for themselves.

Take, for instance, Boy's war service. Davies simply describes what Boy does during the Second World War and lets the reader figure out the significance for himself. Instead of sacrificing during the war, as most people were doing (especially the soldiers who fought and gave their lives in battle), Boy uses the situation for the opposite purpose. He uses the war to further his own success. He takes a post in the Ministry of Food where he can enlist his own corporations on behalf of the country to supply food to soldiers *at a profit to himself*. Thus, by the time Ramsay quietly says that Boy "was now a C.B.E. (for his war work)," the reader knows this is meant to imply that if there is anyone who does *not* deserve such an award, it is Boy.

Next, there is Boy's treatment of Leola and his children. His "work" for the Ministry (which is really for himself) keeps him away from home so much of the time that all three members of his family are neglected. Leola seems to fade away and die from lack of attention. When she is ill and even when she dies, Boy cannot return from England because "duty and the difficulty of transatlantic flights in wartime kept him there." The reader knows, as Ramsay does, that if Boy thought it was important, he would have found a way to return. If flights are so difficult, how did he get to England in the first place? In fact, the reader can only conclude that he has become so callous and unfeeling that the death of his wife is not a matter of importance to him. As for his treatment of David, he finds a way to get rid of him that eases his own conscience. He wants David to be "manly," but Boy's idea of "manly," as we have already seen in Part Four, Chapter 4, is closely tied up with sexual exploits. Certainly, it is not Ramsay's idea of what "manly" means. Putting David in a boys' school from the age of ten on, when he could easily live at home, is heartless and unlikely to make David more "manly" at all.

Finally, Boy's treatment of Ramsay, the friend who has helped him through so much in his life, is ungrateful and petty. When he has the chance to help his friend, he has no trouble firing him from the job he wants even though Ramsay is qualified and has performed successfully under difficult wartime conditions.

In each case, Davies does not accuse Boy of doing anything wrong. He simply dramatizes Boy's egocentric nature in action and lets the reader see through it.

CHAPTER 2

Summary

Ramsay greatly admired the holy picture at the large 19th century Byzantine basilica in Guadalupe. It was not artistically offensive as he had thought it might be. The picture had come from the inside of the cloak of the peasant, Juan Diego, who, in 1531, had gone to Bishop Zumárraga to say that the Virgin Mary had appeared to him several times and had told him to build a shrine in her honour. When the Bishop had been sceptical, the peasant had opened his cloak to show it full of roses in December, and to reveal the painting.

Ramsay examined the painting carefully with his pocket telescope and concluded that it was a skillful depiction of the Immaculate Conception. The Virgin was in the form of a young peasant girl standing on the crescent moon. The proportions were those of a *tilma*, the peasant cloak popular in that area.

Ramsay visited the shrine every day to watch the simple people pray. He thought a great deal about the nature of faith. He could see that these uneducated people sought a reality in the shrine which was symbolically represented by the painting. They were not at all like people in art galleries judging the aesthetic merit of paintings. Ramsay wondered what would happen to this faith once modern education penetrated into their lives. He spent his time writing a prologue to a discussion of the nature of faith, trying to answer this question: "Why do people all over the world, and at all times, want marvels that defy all verifiable facts?" Could it be that all people have an inborn sense that the marvellous is an aspect of the real? Ramsay was not satisfied with the answers philosophers gave to such questions. He was trying to write about it without being either sentimental or too scientific. He was convinced that faith was a psychological reality, and that if it was not given expression in religion to things unseen, it would make trouble with other aspects of life. "The irrational will have its say," he concluded, "perhaps because 'irrational' is the wrong word for it."

When he was not at the shrine, Ramsay slept after lunch and looked around the city before dinner. He had trouble filling the time after dinner. His room made him uncomfortable, mainly because of a painting of the Last Supper which had a lamb looking very much alive laid out on the table staring at Judas. He did not enjoy the Spanish theater because it was dreary. The films were American with Spanish sound tracks. So he was relieved to find that there was a magician called Magnus Eisengrim performing at the Teatro Chueca. Ramsay had never lost his boyhood interest in magic and had seen the best illusionists of his time, including Houdini. He had never heard of Eisengrim whom he thought must be a German who could not return to the United States after the war.

He knew at once that the show would be different from the joking comedies that had become popular as magic shows. Here was a magician who dressed elegantly and took his craft seriously. He gave the impression of mystery with a hint of terror which Ramsay liked best in magic. First, Eisengrim appeared out of nowhere in the middle of the stage and then became transparent while the other members of his company walked through him. Ramsay recognized this as the old Pepper's Ghost illusion.

Eisengrim was not tall, but he had excellent stage presence because of his beautiful eyes and his strong and lovely voice. Ramsay recognized this poetic magician as none other than Paul Dempster. He was amazed, for Eisengrim was unlike the circus conjurer whom he had met in *Le grand Cirque forain de St. Vite* 15 years earlier. Although probably only Ramsay realized it, Eisengrim did no new tricks. They were all classics from the past. But he did them with such style and polish that they seemed like new.

First he poured a number of different drinks from the same bottle, inviting the audience graciously to share with him. Then he did a trick with handkerchiefs, making them disappear, burning them and then making them reappear, all freshly washed. He borrowed a lady's purse, took from it a package which swelled until it became a girl who floated, then he returned her as a small package to the purse. For the second part of the show, he hypnotized about 20 people, even making one of them give an acceptance speech for winning the Nobel Prize. None of the people did anything silly; his hypnosis actually increased their dignity. He went on to demonstrate a number of incredible escapes from ropes and trunks.

The third and last part of the entertainment was serious and erotic. He began with *The Dream of Midas*, an illusion in which he plucked gold coins from the air and from the ears, noses, pockets and hats of people in the audience and threw them into a pot. Next he turned a girl to gold and chipped off one hand and a bit of her face. Relenting, he broke his wand in two. The pot was suddenly empty and the girl flesh again, though bleeding from the stump of one wrist and from the lip. He concluded with *The Vision of Dr. Faustus* which demonstrated the conflict between Sacred and Profane Love. On one side of the stage, the beautiful Faustina posed as Gretchen, sweetly spinning; on the other side, the same Faustina posed nearly naked as Venus. Faust, driven to distraction, killed himself and was dragged down to hell by Mephistopheles, after which Faustina seemed to float above the stage.

The show was a great success. Applause was loud and long. Ramsay tried to go backstage to see Paul, but he was prevented by an usher. Then a large, short-haired woman dressed as a man, the ugliest creature Ramsay had ever seen, asked him if he were Dunstan Ramsay and invited him backstage to see Eisengrim. She was very strong-looking, had big hands and feet, a huge jaw and small deeply-set eyes. But her foreign-sounding voice was beautiful and cultured.

When they got to the dressing room Eisengrim was quarrelling with the naked Faustina about the stage lighting. Faustina threw on a robe, but continued to remove her makeup. She extended a hand to Ramsay who kissed it elegantly. At first Eisengrim was unfriendly, trying to trick Ramsay by switching languages, a trick that didn't fool Ramsay because he too could speak many languages. Paul told him that Le Solitaire died shortly after he had been there and that he had not seen any of the others from the circus since before the war. Ramsay was just about to leave when the large, ugly woman, whose name was Liesl, asked him to come back to lunch the next day. She and Paul quarrelled about this in German, but she won. Then Eisengrim became more friendly and told the others that Ramsay had been his first teacher in magic. He apologized for the "loan" he had made from Ramsay before, explaining that Le Solitaire had been in great need. He tapped Ramsay lightly on the spot where the pocket was in which he carried his money. Later, Ramsay discovered that he had repaid the loan with a little extra. He appreciated this because he liked people to be precise in money matters.

Commentary

In this chapter Davies both states and dramatizes one of the main themes: the difference between "unseen" reality and surface events and the importance of accepting the role of the unseen in human life.

He states this theme through Ramsay who is working on his prologue for "a discussion of the nature of faith." Ramsay ponders the source and meaning of spiritual reality as a result of watching the simple, uneducated peasants of Guadalupe come to worship at their shrine. He makes it very clear that it is not so much for the artistic or cultural aspects of the painting that they come. It is because it represents the possibility for miracles. To Ramsay, too, the painting has a profound meaning which his education and sophistication cannot tarnish. He seriously undertakes to write a book that will be neither an expression of conventional religious beliefs nor a scientific study. The academic discipline which comes closest to his interpretation is psychology. Certainly it is *not* philosophy, which has obscured human understanding of these important truths.

Davies dramatizes the connection between the unseen and the seen in the second half of the chapter by describing the marvels of Eisengrim's magic show. As Ramsay puts it, Eisengrim demonstrates "such visions and illusions as had nourished the imagination of mankind for two thousand years." Davies demonstrates through this magic show the craving man has to believe in marvels and the mysterious, a craving which it is dangerous to deny: "the irrational will have its say, perhaps because 'irrational' is the wrong word for it."

CHAPTER 3

Summary

Soon Ramsay had joined Magnus Eisengrim's company. He never made the tour of South American shrines as planned. At lunch it was all settled among Eisengrim, Liesl and Ramsay.

The beautiful Faustina, according to Eisengrim, was not yet ready to be seen in public places. Ramsay wondered why, since Eisengrim apparently thought it fine to appear in public with the hideous Liesl.

But Liesl seemed less ugly after a while. Her masculine clothes were of excellent quality and her scarf was lovely. She even wore lipstick. Despite her extreme ugliness, she was graceful, intelligent and spoke in a lovely voice.

Eisengrim explained that they were building up a unique magic show in preparation for a world tour. They wished to avoid the type of crude show in which the magician was a comedian. Instead, they wished to create a highly accomplished set of acts to be done with romantic charm, with something like the style of European ballet companies. They wanted to be wondered at. Eisengrim explained that in modern times, art was not fulfilling its proper role of answering the needs of a hungry part of the human spirit. He thought people wanted to marvel at something, and he was setting out to give them satisfaction. It seemed to him that if art did not provide something to wonder at, other more dangerous "wonder-workers," like Hitler, would step in to impress and captivate people.

He planned to discipline the company carefully, making sure that he only appeared under dignified circumstances in public, and that the girls in the company dressed suitably and only accepted invitations from men Eisengrim approved of. Faustina, he explained, was not nearly ready for this: she dressed improperly and ate like an animal. He realized that this would mean that he would have to pay his employees well and that the company would have to be quite small as a result. He added that Liesl was the autocrat of the company and made most of the major decisions. He himself was mainly the magician.

Liesl wanted Ramsay to ghost-write an autobiography of Magnus Eisengrim to enhance the company's reputation. She had read and enjoyed his books about saints and thought that he combined just the right talents to do the kind of book they needed. In the first place, it was to be made up. No one would think much of a magician who came from the family of a Baptist minister in Canada. Liesl also said Ramsay had good taste, the gift of writing delightfully and the ability to convince sceptical readers of the truth of his words.

Ramsay was deeply flattered by Liesl's remarks, especially

her calling him a "distinguished hagiographer." But he was not so flattered that he accepted their terms for payment. He argued that he would need more than the $3500 they offered him. He agreed, however, that he would do it. It seemed like a magnificent adventure to him, and it was surprising, at the age of 50, to have adventures come his way. Now Liesl did not seem ugly to him. He was beginning to appreciate her charm.

Commentary

This chapter advances the plot as Ramsay shifts the course of his life in response to an "adventure." His attitude to life coincides with that of Eisengrim and Liesl, and he is flexible enough to take up the challenge of joining their magic company in order to ghost-write Eisengrim's autobiography.

If this chapter is considered next to Lorne Packer's write-up of Ramsay in the school newspaper, the contrast is striking. Here Ramsay is not in the least a dull, old schoolmaster whose only contribution to society is his teaching. On the contrary, he is a man of considerable talent, as outlined by Liesl, who has spent his free time on great spiritual adventures of which his colleagues at Colborne College could have no knowledge. This chapter, among others, provides a strong argument to the Headmaster that Packer's assessment has been inaccurate and insulting. Furthermore, it substantiates Ramsay's claim to having played the role of Fifth Business. In setting out to ghost-write a fictional autobiography for Eisengrim, he once again plays a "vital, though never glorious" role in relation to his boyhood friend, Paul Dempster.

CHAPTER 4

Summary

A month later, Ramsay was sick of the magic company, but it was as if they had cast a spell on him which he was powerless to break.

He found it flattering to sit with Liesl in the theater watching Eisengrim practise his tricks. He was a real master of the art, and worked hard to perfect each act. Ramsay was asked to give his opinion about parts of the show and he did. He suggested that Eisengrim drop the escape acts because they were not romantic enough. When Liesl suggested including an act called *The Brazen Head of Friar Bacon*, Ramsay supported her.

Ramsay wrote the speech Eisengrim would use to tell about the great priest-magician who could foretell the future and knew the past. It was a good thought-reading act in which the Brazen Head (made by Liesl) was floated over the stage by Eisengrim. Girls would collect objects from people in the audience, put them in envelopes and then Eisengrim would "read" what was in them. The Brazen Head would also give messages to three random members of the audience about their personal affairs. This last trick was accomplished by having the company manager pick the pockets of three people as they came into the theater so that Liesl could deduce from letters and other materials something about their private lives. Because of one message from the Brazen Head, a duel had been fought which gave this act a great deal of publicity. Ramsay opposed the idea of putting it at the end of the show; he liked Dr. Faustus better for that purpose. Ramsay also gave Eisengrim the idea of sawing a member of the audience in half. This was accomplished by hypnotism.

Although Ramsay loved working on all these illusions, he sensed that it was destroying his character. He felt like a child again. His imagination was given free range, he began to lie and to become egotistic and boastful. When he slapped one of the showgirls on the bottom one day, he knew something was wrong with him. He never would have done such a thing before. He had become an indiscreet talker, unable to keep secrets, especially from Liesl, and he had fallen in love with Faustina.

Liesl, he discovered, was from a Swiss family of wealthy watchmakers. Her money backed the company and she was also the company mechanic. Somehow, she was able to get Ramsay to talk freely to her. He told her all about the autobiography of Eisengrim as he was writing it, something he never would have done before because he superstitiously believed that no author should talk about a book until it was finished. Ramsay was making Paul into a northern wizard who had been born into a distinguished family of Danes or Swedes in Finland. His wolf-like name had supposedly been assumed in tribute to the savage animals. Ramsay enhanced this basic plot with material drawn from his knowledge of the northern saints.

Liesl told Ramsay that he was better off to tell his secrets, even though it made him uncomfortable. She thought he had been "buttoned-up" too long. She knew Ramsay despised her. In fact, she thought he despised almost everyone because he had put all his affection into Mrs. Dempster instead of spreading it among the people he knew. She thought that Deptford was a horrid place and that his Scots family had made him a "moral monster."

Ramsay was infatuated with Faustina, even though he realized that she was totally unsuitable for him. She lived like an animal and was stupid and conceited. Furthermore, she was 30 years younger than he was. But he couldn't help hanging around for a glimpse of her changing during the magic show, and some nights he thought of little else. This infatuation even made him wonder whether education was a worthwhile venture as he had always believed. One evening, she called him "St. Ramsay" and wiggled her hips at him. Ramsay knew that she was officially Eisengrim's mistress; at least they shared a room. But he thought that Eisengrim was so egotistic that perhaps he didn't pay much attention to her. His hopes that there might be a chance that he could have her were dashed one evening when he saw Liesl and Faustina in an intimate sexual embrace. His spirit collapsed.

Commentary

Giving in to his impulse to join Eisengrim's company leads to some profound changes in Ramsay's character. As Ramsay himself confesses, "I could not control myself." The character he has spent such a long time building up as schoolmaster, historian and hagiographer seems to be disintegrating. Other aspects of his character which have had to be sacrificed so that he could attain his goals in life now assert themselves. Where before he was "close-mouthed" and "never betrayed a confidence," he is now a "chatterbox" who tells Liesl everything about his past "like a magpie." Whereas he has been "a bachelor of unstained character," he now falls ridiculously in love with an "animal" of a girl. Where he has been "a figure of authority, of scholarship, of probity," he now develops "the absorbing egotism of a child."

Davies here demonstrates the psychological phenomenon explored by his favourite psychologist, Jung, which is sometimes called the "mid-life crisis." Ramsay, in mid-life, must "let go" of the rigid self-discipline which has enabled him to pursue his course in life. The aspects of character he has kept under control now burst forth in a way that is almost ridiculous. As Liesl comments, however, such a righting of the balance is necessary if Ramsay is going to "enjoy a few years of almost normal humanity." Even though he is 50, Ramsay learns something new about himself.

CHAPTER 5

Summary

Liesl knocked on Ramsay's door about one a.m. in her pyjamas and dressing gown. She wanted to talk to him. She explained that she had noticed Ramsay in a mirror when he had seen her with Faustina and she felt sorry for him. He seemed to her like a man "whose bottled-up feelings have burst their bottle and splashed glass and acid everywhere."

Ramsay thought it was undignified for him to be spoken to like this by Liesl. He said he was only trying to be decent and honest so that he didn't take advantage of helpless people.

Liesl said that if he meant Faustina, he was wrong. He didn't understand her. Liesl explained that Faustina was a very earthy creature whose physical life was her entire existence. It would be her destiny to be glorious for a few years, not to marry someone like him. She thought Ramsay viewed life as a spectator sport, afraid to get involved. Now that his feelings were involved, he was having a rough time. He had not understood he must court Faustina with presents and food.

Ramsay protested that he would not be an interesting physical partner for Faustina. Liesl disagreed. She went on to ask Ramsay if he would like to go to bed now with her. Ramsay was astonished. He began to walk towards the door, but Liesl grabbed his pyjama coat and pulled him back to the bed, concluding that he wanted her to be aggressive in lovemaking. She was strong and supple and tried to kiss him with her monkey-like mouth, but Ramsay fought back and threw her on the floor with a crash. Then Liesl grabbed his wooden leg from the corner of the room and hit him across the shin. Ramsay took it from her and cornered her. He dropped the leg and punched her fiercely in anger. She was crying and blood dripped from her cut lip. Catching her as she made for the door, Ramsay took her nose in his fingers and twisted it until it cracked. Finally, she escaped out the door.

Afterwards, Ramsay felt much better. He felt as if his reason was returning. He was suddenly hungry, for he had eaten no dinner. He took out a flask of whisky and drank a little.

There was a tap on the door. The Spanish man from downstairs, who had earlier thumped the ceiling when he heard so much noise, was asking him to be more quiet. He thought Ramsay and Liesl were on their honeymoon. Soon there was another knock on the door. It was Liesl asking for her key. Ramsay asked her in, offered her a drink of whisky and helped wash her cuts and bruises. Soon they were sitting in bed together, taking turns with the whisky. Liesl explained that she had come in the first place simply to tell Ramsay that he was human like other people. She said that knowing what she did of his life, she could see that he had made himself responsible for other people's troubles. He was decent to everyone but himself. She explained that his Calvinist upbringing had taught him a cruel way of life. What had happened to him recently was "the revenge of the unlived life," she said. There had been a whole part of his life that had been set aside; now it had made a fool of him.

Liesl went on to tell him to look carefully at that unlived part of his life. Every man has a personal devil, she warned. Ramsay must become acquainted with his. In addition, he must get to know the devil himself. Christians who tried to take God out of their religion and keep everything else were the worst off, she claimed. They ended up with a cruel doctrine without the "poetic grace of myth."

Liesl offered him some advice. It was advice not for everyone, but for the "twice-born" like Ramsay, who had assumed another name from Diana Marfleet. She told him to do something irrational at the devil's bidding, just for the hell of it. She added that he would one day understand the meaning of her name.

Liesl said that she thought Ramsay was Fifth Business. That was the way in which he fit into poetry and myth. She explained who Fifth Business was in the old opera companies. Although he is the one who has no partner of the opposite sex, as the hero, the heroine, the sorceress or the villain did, his role was important. He was the one who made the plot work. He perhaps knew the secret of the hero's birth, came to the assistance of the heroine or could even be the cause of someone's death. Those who play this role, she went on, sometimes have a career that lasts longer than that of the more spectacular characters.

Ramsay adds, for the Headmaster's benefit, that he has

altered the report a little, tidying Liesl's English and condensing what she said. But the two of them talked until about four, made love and fell asleep.

The next morning there was a note from the Spaniard downstairs tied to his door with a bunch of flowers. It asked his forgiveness and wished him many happy nights with his new wife.

Commentary

In this final chapter of Part Five, it becomes clear why the chapter has been titled "Liesl." It is Liesl who names and helps fulfil Ramsay's destiny. In Part Two, Chapter 6, Diana Marfleet renamed him Dunstan after St. Dunstan who was tempted by the Devil in the shape of a fascinating woman. Like St. Dunstan, Ramsay is now tempted by Lieslotte Vitzlipützli whose last name comes from one of the devils in Goethe's play *Faust*. Her "temptation" is not simply the attempt she makes to seduce him, which he at first successfully rejects, as the original St. Dunstan did, by twisting her nose. It is the temptation to do something "irrational." This is a particularly appropriate temptation for Dunstan Ramsay, for he has patterned his life along principles of strict reason and decency. Now, his "unlived life" of the emotions bursts forth to tempt him to act unreasonably. For a long time he has repressed his feelings in an inhuman way, but now they take over, under the encouragement of the intelligent and intuitive Liesl, to make a fool of him. Like St. Dunstan, however, he resists temptation. He goes beyond it to learn something about himself.

Liesl is also an important figure in Ramsay's life because it is she who first tells him that his role is that of Fifth Business. Liesl explains for Ramsay what this means and shows him the value of having this destiny.

PART SIX • CHAPTER 1

Summary

Ramsay enjoyed writing Eisengrim's autobiography because he could let himself go and invent the kind of story about magic that he would have enjoyed as a child. Because it was full of romance and marvels with an undertone of eroticism and sadism, it sold extremely well. People loved to read about how hard Eisengrim worked preparing his acts, how lovely women pursued him, how his workshop was located in a Tyrolean castle and how girls sometimes were hurt in practice. Ramsay made him a bit of a monster and left his age a vague matter. The book brought him a small annual income from then on.

Ramsay went to the Adirondacks in New York to finish writing this book a few days after his dramatic encounter with Liesl. Meanwhile, Eisengrim's show was going to tour Central America before going to Europe. Ramsay gave Faustina a necklace and she kissed him in return. He gave Eisengrim an expensive set of studs and cufflinks for his evening dress. Then he persuaded him to send money regularly to help support his mother, Mrs. Dempster. He gave nothing to Liesl because they had become extremely close friends.

Ramsay was pleased to have some financial help with Mrs. Dempster from her son. Eisengrim's monthly cheques covered about one-third of the cost of keeping her in the hospital near a small town where Ramsay had moved her after the war. Conditions there were a great improvement: she was a private patient, she had some company if she wanted it and she could take walks in the pleasant surroundings. Although Ramsay wanted to do the right thing, and did look after her, he resented the expense which meant that he had to deny himself.

One day he made a dreadful mistake: he told her about Paul. Although she had become old and white-haired, her face was unlined and she had regained that sweet expression from her Deptford days. When she heard about Paul, however, she became very agitated and excited. To her, Paul was still a lost, little boy. She even imagined that he had been kidnapped by gypsies. When Ramsay said he had seen Paul, she concluded that Ramsay must be keeping him from her. She would not listen to Ramsay's explanation that Paul was now over 40 and sent his love. As she became more excited, Ramsay made more mistakes. He told her that Paul was helping support her. Then he told her that Paul was supporting her entirely. This only convinced her that Ramsay was a villain, keeping her apart from her son.

She rushed at Ramsay, tried to scratch his eyes and began to scream. A nurse came running and helped Ramsay calm her down. But she had to be kept strapped down and was given a needle to quiet her.

Officials at the hospital told Ramsay within a week that he should not visit her anymore. She was kept in a room with barred windows.

Commentary

This scene is highly ironic. Whereas Ramsay, all his grown life, has revered Mrs. Dempster to the point of worshipping her as a saint, she now turns on him and thinks of him as just the opposite: "an enemy, an undoubted agent of those dark forces who had torn Paul from her." The contrast between his reverence for her which "was so great that I could not bear to be rough with her" and her confused and violent attack on him as she "tried to scratch my eyes" is deeply pathetic. Even her rejection of him cannot cause Ramsay to change his view of her.

CHAPTER 2

Summary

Ramsay was not only depressed about the change in his relationship with Mrs. Dempster, but he also lost touch with Boy Staunton when he remarried. Boy's new wife did not like Ramsay.

During the war, Boy had developed a taste for politics. He was a Conservative who had been elected at a time when the Liberals did not nominate anyone to oppose him because they planned on a coalition government. Boy saw himself as a hero who would rescue Canadians from the tyrannical Liberals, and he intended to apply business methods to accomplish this. Both these views betrayed the fact that he was an amateur in politics.

Everything about Boy was wrong for politics: he was rich, handsome and had no political friends. In spite of this, he was elected once, but he made some silly speeches in the House of Commons and abused the newspapers which was politically unwise.

He had some loyal supporters, among them Denyse
Hornick. She had been a very capable lieutenant commander in
the W.R.N.S. during the war. Afterwards, she had opened a
small travel agency and made it into a large one. It seemed to
Ramsay that she tricked Boy into marrying her.

Ramsay doubted whether Boy understood women apart
from their sexuality. He was attracted to Denyse because she
was in a few groups that worked for women in public life. The
best compliment he could pay her was that she had "a masculine mind."

At the next election, Boy was defeated decisively because
he often criticized his own party and he had offended the newspapers. He also bullied his electors. Denyse remained his most
faithful supporter because she had a plan to make him Lieutenant-Governor of the Province of Ontario.

The holder of this office was named by the Dominion
Cabinet, and there were never many candidates because it cost
quite a bit of money to maintain the lifestyle. It would be at
least five years before a new appointment would be made, which
gave Denyse enough time to plan Boy's campaign carefully. Boy
thought this a good idea. The only thing he lacked was a wife.
But Denyse cleverly manipulated him until it dawned on him
that she would be the perfect woman to help him.

At first, she pretended that she had no interest in marrying
him. She argued that since she was divorced, she would not be a
suitable wife for a Lieutenant-Governor. Next, she pleaded that
she had been involved with other men since her divorce. Then
she said that people might think that she had married him for
his money. Finally, she claimed that she was just a small-town
girl who probably would not be able to handle the social
requirements of the job. To all her objections, Boy argued that
none of these things should make any difference. Denyse
admitted that she loved him and had always known that he was
a proud and great man.

Their wedding was more a "function" than a celebration
or a religious occasion. Between them, they gathered a lot of
important people together, talked the bishop into overlooking
Denyse's divorce, and saw to it that the very best champagne
and food were served. David and Caroline were rude and
hostile. They not only disliked Denyse, they could not stand
Denyse's daughter Lorene. Lorene was a short, heavy 13-year-
old who wore thick glasses and tripped over everything. When

she laughed loudly, she drooled. She attended a special boarding school where she was learning to cook and sew because she could not handle academic subjects. She was the clown at the wedding and eventually she got so drunk she fell over. Ramsay had to take her into an anteroom where she told him all about how clever her dog was before she fell asleep.

Commentary

Boy continues to live a dreadful life into late middle age. He is older now, but no wiser. Davies shows two areas of life in which he is naive: politics and love.

In politics, Boy has no idea what is and is not important. To take only one example, he offends the newspapers by insulting them in the Commons during his first term as an M.P. Later, the newspapers are partly to blame in his defeat at the next election.

In love, he has such a simple view of women — as sexual objects — that when he meets an intelligent and determined woman like Denyse Hornick, he can't see that she is manipulating him and using him for her own purposes. Because he has no real moral principles, he is unable to assess the real obstacles to the success of the marriage, which Denyse herself cleverly raises so that she cannot later be blamed for any of them by Boy.

In contrast to Ramsay, who has undergone his own "midlife crisis" and learned much about himself in the process, Boy has stopped developing as a human being long ago.

CHAPTER 3

Summary

Denyse had the usual dislike a woman has for the friends her husband made before he married her. She especially did not like Ramsay. She was not just uninterested in spiritual matters, she was strongly opposed to them. The only reason she had agreed to have a church wedding was that Boy's position seemed to demand it. She was actually an atheist who condemned the church ceremony because it put women at a disadvantage. She spent her abundant energy on women's causes: easier divorce, equal pay for equal work and so on. She was "reasonable, logical and untiring" in pursuing these aims.

Boy confided to Ramsay that Denyse was really just a shy

kid who needed affection and sex, but Ramsay never saw that side of her. She sensed that he cared about women for the very things she thought women should overcome. Furthermore, she knew about his interest in saints and religion and, whenever he dropped in to see Boy, she would pick a fight with him about these subjects.

Boy, who was richer and more important than ever, tried to help by asking Ramsay to have lunch at his club sometimes. He was still handsome and magnetic, but when he was relaxing, he seemed grim and disillusioned. He had taken up Denyse's "rationalism" and one day, after the mixed reviews of Ramsay's book on the psychology of myth and legend had come out, he accused Ramsay of being trivial-minded and of encouraging superstition. Ramsay was angry with him, so Boy excused himself by saying that he didn't like the stuff Ramsay wrote because he was an atheist. Ramsay replied, "I'm not surprised. You created a God in your own image, and when you found out he was no good you abolished him. It's a quite common form of psychological suicide."

To Ramsay's surprise, this remark seemed to affect Boy deeply. He said that he felt rotten because now that he'd done everything he set out to do, everyone thought he was a success. But he wished he could just climb into a car and drive away from everything, even though he knew that he was lucky to have Denyse.

Ramsay explained to him that this was really a mythological wish. It was like King Arthur's passing into the next world wearing his armour. He pointed out that Boy could not do that. He would have to grow old. Boy looked at him with hate in his eyes and said that was crazy, defeatist nonsense. But, soon, he was genial again.

Ramsay was worried about him. As a boy he had been a bully, a boaster and a bad loser. As an adult, he had learned how to cover this up, but Ramsay thought boyhood traits did not just disappear, and he suspected that, as Boy got older, he would be more and more as he used to be. Certainly Ramsay himself was getting that way. He used to get off "good ones" as a boy, and now he was becoming a sharp-tongued old man. As they both neared their 60s, their essential selves were coming closer to the surface.

Commentary

Davies returns to the theme of the changes that take place in mid-life. Here he theorizes that "the traits that are strong in childhood . . . very often make a vigorous appearance after the meridian of life has been passed."

Again, Ramsay and Boy are compared. Ramsay's boyhood nature has come to the surface in late middle age: he is as sharp-tongued now as he was then. But the traits that Boy displayed in childhood are more dangerous. In the opening scene, the reader saw how angry and violent he could be over a small matter. Now that much more is at stake (for example, his plan to become Lieutenant-Governor of Ontario), the unleashing of those boyhood traits could have disastrous consequences. What Boy has always had and may not now conceal is "his naked wish to dominate everybody" and his tendency to get "angry and ugly when things went against him."

CHAPTER 4

Summary

Mrs. Dempster died the year after Boy's second marriage. This surprised Ramsay who had expected her to live longer than he did. It was his stupid talk about Paul that affected her. Also, it may have been the fact that he asked that she be sedated as little as possible. This made her care more expensive and allowed her to go into fits of rage at Ramsay. She thought he had caused all her trouble.

She also developed physical problems: slight diabetes and a weak kidney and heart. Ramsay knew she was breaking up. Even so, he was surprised when the hospital called to tell him to come because she had had a heart attack. He sat with her in the infirmary. She was unconscious but, after a while, she came to and asked him if he were Dunstable Ramsay. When he answered "yes," she said that it was strange because she thought Dunstable Ramsay was a boy. After that she was unconscious for about an hour, gave his hand a little squeeze and died.

Ramsay had a terrible reaction to her death. He wept for the first time since his mother had chased him around screaming when he was a boy. He hardly slept all night. The next morning he cut himself shaving, threw up his breakfast and was hard on a stupid boy in his class.

He had arranged to have the body sent to Toronto to be

cremated. The day after her death, he went to the undertaker's. Although she was heavily made up, she looked like an old woman ready for burial. Ramsay knelt and prayed in a vague way for her salvation, and then he begged forgiveness for himself for all the ways in which he had mismanaged his care of her. Then he did a strange thing. He knew that, traditionally, saints smelled sweet like violets after death. He still thought of her as a saint, so he leaned over to sniff. But she only smelled of perfume put on by the undertaker who, at that moment, came in and explained that it was Chanel Number Five that he had used. The undertaker thought that Ramsay was Mrs. Dempster's son, but Ramsay denied it. He also denied that she was his aunt, without explaining who she was. "Friend" seemed inadequate for all she had meant to him.

The following day he sat alone in the crematory chapel as the body went into the flames. No one else remembered her.

Commentary

In describing the death of Mrs. Dempster, Davies begins to bring his complicated plot to an end. But the death of Mrs. Dempster is most remarkable for its effect upon Ramsay. He says, "It gave me a clutching around my own heart that scared me" when he hears of her heart attack. After her death, he goes to pieces, feeling that what has happened is "a terrible invasion of the spirit." Whatever Mrs. Dempster has meant to him, it has been like a part of his own soul, and her death is like the end of some aspect of himself.

CHAPTER 5

Summary

Mrs. Dempster died in March. The following summer Ramsay was off to Europe to visit the Bollandists, hoping that they would praise his latest book. They did praise it, and happened to mention that Padre Blazon was still alive in a hospital in Vienna. Ramsay set off to see him.

Blazon was not changed much, except for the fact that his few teeth were now gone. He still wore his old velvet skullcap on his wild, white hair. He recognized Ramsay at once and asked him his age. Ramsay replied that he was 61. Blazon refused to give his exact age, but admitted he was over 100. He praised Ramsay's book which he had asked a nun in the hospital to read until he could no longer stand her accent. After that, he had made her read the anticlerical book, *Le Juif errant*, to him so he could enjoy her discomfort.

To Blazon's inquiry about his "fool-saint," Ramsay explained what had happened. Blazon told him of the recent canonization of Bertilla Boscardin, a woman who had worked wonders with hospital patients during the First World War. On the nurse's suggestion, the next time he visited Blazon, he brought him some Viennese chocolate in a little box with special tongs for picking up the chocolates. When he saw the tongs, Blazon said, "Aha, St. Dunstan and his tongs!" and asked Ramsay to bring him some wine too, if he could.

Blazon had been thinking about Mrs. Dempster and had concluded that as a saint she never would have been approved by the Bollandists. However, he said that Ramsay would be quite right to pray for her on All Saints' Day because she had lived a heroic life like other saints. He went on to ask Ramsay if he had met the Devil yet? Ramsay told him all about his encounter with Liesl in Mexico City. Blazon agreed that an encounter with the Devil might be a beneficial experience, especially for someone like Ramsay who was prepared to meet him on equal terms. To him, Ramsay's encounter with Liesl was a re-enactment of St. Dunstan's seizing the Devil's nose with his tongs.

Ramsay asked him whether he had found a God to teach him how to be old. Blazon replied that he had, and that this God was calm and quiet, but very much alive. "We *do*," he said, "but He *is*." Ramsay left him laughing and pinching his big nose with the tiny chocolate tongs.

Ramsay spent a week in Salzburg sightseeing. To his great surprise, he finally found the statue of the little Madonna which he had once seen on the battlefield in France. It was part of a private collection in a display called Schöne Madonnen in the exhibition rooms of the Cathedral. On close inspection, her face was not that of Mrs. Dempster after all, but her expression was very similar to the look of mercy and love, tempered with perception, that Ramsay remembered. Every day Ramsay visited the display to look at the Madonna. Although he could not take a picture, because photographs were not allowed, her image would stay with him forever.

Commentary

This scene concludes the portion of the plot which concerns Ramsay's search for the meaning of sainthood. First of all, he receives his due praise from the expert Bollandists for his "big book" on saints. His life work has borne fruit.

Secondly, he sees Padre Blazon again for the last time and receives final religious guidance when Blazon tells him about finding the God who can help one be old. He is a God who *is*, not one who can *do*.

Blazon also tells him how to deal with his desire to make a saint of Mrs. Dempster. The important thing is not whether she is a saint (although since her life has been one of heroic endurance, it will not be blasphemous to worship her as a saint on All Saints' Day), but what her life has meant in relation to Ramsay's. Belief in her has "coloured your life with beauty and goodness," Blazon observes. "Too much scientizing will not help you." Instead of trying to make a saint of Mrs. Dempster, a task which is hopeless because the Bollandists would never accept her, Ramsay should be satisfied to contemplate the rich meaning her life has held for him.

Finally, Ramsay finds the little Madonna he had tried to find after Passchendaele. Significantly, he finds her "after having abandoned hope and forgotten my search." In other words, it is not by man's willpower that revelation comes but, more mysteriously, when the time is ripe.

CHAPTER 6

Summary

Boy Staunton's death was sensational. Ramsay reminds the Headmaster of the details. It was about 4 o'clock on the morning of November 4, 1968, when his Cadillac convertible was dredged up from the Toronto harbour. It had been driven very fast off the end of the concrete pier. There was one odd detail: Boy had a stone in his mouth, an ordinary piece of pinkish granite about the size of an egg.

The newspapers wrote it up. Was it murder? But how could anyone want to murder someone who had done so much for the nation? Was it suicide? But why would the head of Alpha Corporation, one of the richest men in Canada, handsome and still youthful-looking, want to kill himself? His home life was wonderful, and within a few days it would have been announced that he was to be the next Lieutenant-Governor of Ontario.

Many people sent tributes. Even Joel Surgeoner, whose Mission Boy had supported. There was a brief mention of his first wife and her death in 1942. Lorene was mentioned before either David (now about 40, a lawyer and often drunk) and Caroline (now Mrs. Beeston Bastable, with a daughter called Caroline).

Denyse did her best to arrange a state funeral, but there was no flag on the coffin and no soldiers were in attendance. She did manage to get a number of important people to attend, and Bishop Woodiwiss spoke in tribute to Boy, though he mumbled.

There was one thing in which she did not succeed. She rudely asked Ramsay to write an "official" life of Boy Staunton, but Ramsay refused. Ramsay had a heart attack which allowed him to turn this down, along with several other things he didn't want to do. He seriously wondered whether he could write the life story of Boy anyway. He now knew how relative truth could be.

Ramsay adds to the Headmaster that this memoir will not be released until after his death. Then the Headmaster can decide how much of the truth he wants to make public. It will not make any legal difference because he will not be able to prove anything.

Commentary

As the memoir draws to a close, Davies uses a clever device to provide factual information the reader needs to tie up some of the loose ends of the plot.

He puts information about the sensational death of Boy Staunton in the form of a newspaper report. It is natural that a newspaper would report on the death of an important person like Boy, and it is even more likely when the circumstances are so dramatic. In addition to the speculation about Boy's death, moreover, the reader obtains information about a number of other characters. David is now 40 and an alcoholic lawyer. Caroline has married and has a daughter. Joel Surgeoner is still running his Mission. Denyse's long-range plan to have Boy appointed Lieutenant-Governor of Ontario has succeeded.

CHAPTER 7

Summary

Magnus Eisengrim came to Canada in 1968 for two weeks at the end of October, after becoming so famous that his picture was on the cover of *Time* as the world's greatest magician in history. The *Autobiography* sold well in Canada. No one guessed that both its subject and its author were native-born.

Faustina had been replaced by another beautiful girl with the same name. Liesl was now in early middle age and, as with Blazon, Ramsay continued his conversations with her as if they had never been apart.

Ramsay arranged for Eisengrim to come to the school to talk to the boys about hypnotism. Eisengrim explained that no one would do anything under hypnosis that they would not do ordinarily or had not wished to do at some time. He hypnotized Ramsay and had him make up a poem.

After the talk, Ramsay and Eisengrim were walking past the Headmaster's study when out came Boy Staunton. Boy recognized Eisengrim because he had taken Lorene to see the magic show as a birthday treat, and Eisengrim had given her a box of candy. Eisengrim remembered the very seat and row she was in, and could also describe Lorene. Boy asked how the Brazen Head could have known a bit of local scandal that afterwards caused gossip. Eisengrim refused to tell him, but noticed that Boy's question meant that he must have come back the following night. He mentioned that he could have released the information about Boy's upcoming appointment, but decided against it. Boy responded that Eisengrim couldn't have known, because he had only received his letter a couple of hours before going to the theater. Eisengrim observed that Boy had the letter with him right then. He went on to explain that he could see the corner of a creamy envelope such as would only be used by the government. Boy admitted he had just shown it to the Headmaster as an explanation for resigning from the Board of Governors. He was on his way to tell Dunny about it.

Ramsay invited Boy to join Eisengrim and himself for a drink. Boy, realizing it had been a blunder to ask Eisengrim how the Brazen Head worked, tried now to be especially charming. His method was to be insulting to Ramsay. Ramsay was intensely curious to see what would happen next because he could see that very strong feelings had arisen between Eisengrim and Boy, feelings of the kind that can lead to deep friendship or strong hatred. They went to Ramsay's room, which Boy criticized for its untidiness. Eisengrim responded by saying it looked like a room where there was "peace and a mind at work." Boy went on to insult Ramsay's work, but Eisengrim defended him. Ramsay had a certain pleasure in knowing who Eisengrim really was when Boy didn't.

Eisengrim said that he had come from Deptford and went on to explain that Ramsay had written the *Autobiography*. He told Boy that his real name was Paul Dempster and that Ramsay had been an old friend, initiating him into magic. He continued to tell them about his running away from home to join the carnival. He had been entranced by Willard the Wizard, a conjurer who had a weakness for boys and morphia. In exchange for sexual favours, Willard taught Paul many tricks. It was his craving for morphia that ruined him. In order to raise money to buy it, he took to "geeking" which was a special act in which a man ate live creatures. It had to be done without the authorities finding out. Eventually there was trouble with the police, and the company went abroad, finally ending up in the Tyrol where Ramsay had first encountered them. Paul explained that he had not left the circus because he felt loyal to Willard in much the same way that Ramsay had felt loyal to Mrs. Dempster.

Eisengrim went on to explain that he could not be loyal to his mother because she had been responsible for his suffering. His birth had robbed her of her sanity, and her acts had led to endless teasing about "hoors" that he had endured from people like Boy. Paul had edited his memories down to incidents of pain and cruelty.

Boy did not remember anything about the Dempsters or the snowball. Eisengrim explained that his patron, Liesl, had given him his name and that it meant Wolf. "You," he said to Boy, "have chosen forever to be a Boy." He revealed that Ramsay had long ago told him that Staunton's mother had nicknamed him "Pidgy Boy-Boy." Here was something Ramsay had edited out of his memories. He protested, but Eisengrim said something that applied to all three of them, "We all forget many of the things we do, especially when they do not fit into the character we have chosen for ourselves."

Ramsay explained that he had been renamed when he broke away from his mother. Paul remembered Mrs. Ramsay as a hard woman, but Ramsay told him that it had been she who had kept him alive.

Boy took down what he thought was a cigar case from a shelf. It was a box containing the ashes of Mrs. Dempster, and it said on a plaque:

Requiescat in pace
MARY DEMPSTER
1888-1959
Here is the patience
and faith of the saints.

Ramsay explained that he had kept it because he felt guilty about her, revered her and had not found a suitable place for it.

Eisengrim asked why he felt guilty. Ramsay might have kept silent but, seeing himself as Fifth Business, he told them the story of the snowball. Boy protested that Ramsay had made a mountain of a molehill. But Ramsay, feeling even more like Fifth Business, went on. He picked up his pink granite paperweight and handed it to Boy, explaining that it was the very stone Boy had hidden in the snowball that had hit Mrs. Dempster. He told Boy that it was time he faced the truth about himself. The stone-in-the-snowball had always been characteristic of his behaviour.

Boy turned on Ramsay and accused him of being ungrateful for all his financial help. Ramsay replied that it was time Boy started trying to be a human being. Perhaps then he would see that there were things in life more important than himself.

Eisengrim rose to leave, saying that Sundays were the only night he could get to bed before midnight. Boy offered to give him a ride to his hotel. Ramsay asked Eisengrim if he would like to take his mother's ashes. "No thanks, Ramsay," was his odd reply, "I have everything I need."

It was not until after the news of Boy's death reached Ramsay the next morning that he noticed his paperweight was gone.

Commentary

This chapter is the climax of the novel. In it, Ramsay fulfils his destiny as Fifth Business. For the first time since Paul's premature birth, the three men whose fates are intertwined are together in the same room: Boy, whose snowball caused Mrs. Dempster's tragedy; Eisengrim, the magician who was born and suffered as a result; and Ramsay for whom the snowball was intended. But only Ramsay has the information necessary to bring the true story to light. He knew who threw the snowball, he saw and understood what it did to Mrs. Dempster. He found and kept the stone that Boy had hidden in the snowball and he knows that Eisengrim is really Paul Dempster. Without any of these pieces of information — especially considering the way each man has revised his past to suit the present — the truth could not come to light and the plot would not be resolved.

As is fitting in the climax of the story, the scene is one of heightened emotion. Not only is there the intense emotion that Ramsay notices between Boy and Eisengrim, but there is resentment on Paul's part, anger from Boy and even disillusionment for himself.

CHAPTER 8

Summary

Police investigations and Denyse's delays postponed the funeral until Thursday. The following Saturday, Ramsay went to the Royal Alexandra Theatre to see Eisengrim's show. Most of the time he spent backstage with Liesl, but he stood behind a curtain in one of the boxes, during *The Brazen Head of Friar Bacon*, to watch the audience.

Everything went smoothly until it came time for the Head to give its messages to various members of the audience. After Eisengrim had said what was to come, a voice from the top balcony yelled out: "Who killed Boy Staunton?" Liesl's voice came through the Head:

"He was killed by the usual cabal: by himself, first of all; by the woman he knew; by the woman he did not know; by the man who granted his inmost wish; and by the inevitable fifth, who was keeper of his conscience and keeper of the stone."

This caused an uproar. Denyse thought she must be "the woman he knew" and hounded the police to do something to get rid of Eisengrim, but he and his troupe had already flown to Copenhagen. Ramsay knew nothing that happened afterwards because he had a heart attack and was rushed to the hospital. When he was well enough to read, he was given a postcard from

Liesl that said she was sorry about his illness which was partly her fault. She invited him to come to Switzerland to join her and the Brazen Head.

And that, Ramsay added to the Headmaster, was all he had to tell.

Commentary

Davies concludes his story with the heart attack and the invitation that takes Ramsay to Switzerland where he is writing his memoirs. As for the mystery of Boy's death, he leaves the reader with a riddle that has many possible answers. In that way, he gives a final sense of mystery to his story as an example of what his book has demonstrated all along: that people have a need for mysteries in their lives.

Character Sketches

Dunstan Ramsay

As a boy, Dunstan Ramsay is big for his age and clumsy. As a man, he has "a cadaverous and scowling cast of countenance and a rather pedantic Scots voice."

Ramsay has many characteristics that make him a good narrator. From the beginning of his story, he is a precise and careful observer: "My lifelong involvement with Mrs. Dempster began at 5:58 o'clock p.m. on 27 December 1908, at which time I was ten years and seven months old." Throughout the long memoir he writes to his Headmaster, he deliberately tries to be accurate. In addition, Ramsay is a born storyteller. Even as a boy, he reads stories about saints to keep little Paul Dempster happy so that he will continue to provide an audience for his magic tricks. Later, when Ramsay visits Mrs. Dempster in the mental institution, Ramsay tells stories to the inmates to keep them happy.

Ramsay is brought up in an intellectual Scottish Presbyterian family in Deptford. This upbringing forms him to a great extent, making him feel excessive guilt throughout his life and encouraging him to repress his emotions. Like his father, the owner and editor of the *Deptford Banner*, Ramsay is exceptionally intelligent. Unlike his father, Ramsay is too clumsy to manage the skills necessary to produce a newspaper. This clumsiness prevents Ramsay from taking over his father's paper and from becoming the magician he would like to be. The strong willpower he has inherited from his mother enables him to stand up to his parents and leave home to enlist as a soldier in the First World War.

His final break from his parents — especially his mother — occurs when he refuses to marry Diana Marfleet, the English nurse who looks after him until he is able to walk on his artificial leg after the war. When she renames him "Dunstan" after St. Dunstan, and he gives up his mother's maiden name of "Dunstable," he becomes one of the "twice-born," symbolically leaving Deptford behind him and beginning a new life.

The strongest aspect of Ramsay's personality is his intelligence, so after the war, in which he is bored except for reading the New Testament, he enrols at the University of Toronto and obtains both a B.A. and M.A. in History.

On completing his education, Ramsay takes a position as a

teacher in Colborne College, a private boys' school in Toronto. But his real career is not teaching. Because of his interest in spiritual matters, he is attracted to a special branch of history called hagiography. Studying saints is his passion from that point on, and he travels widely in pursuit of the information that eventually finds its way into his books: *A Hundred Saints for Travellers, Forgotten Saints of the Tyrol, Celtic Saints of Britain and Europe* and *The Saints: A Study in History and Popular Mythology*. He also writes articles for the *Analecta Bollandiana*.

As a boy, Ramsay sensed that *Arabian Nights* and the Bible were similar. His most important life's work consists of an exploration of this idea until he understands that "the marvellous is an aspect of the real." Ramsay's quest to understand the mysterious dimension in life takes him into the realms of conventional religion, art history, pagan myth and the marvellous shows of the greatest magicians of his age.

From boyhood, moreover, his spiritual quest operates on a personal level as well as an intellectual level. From the time when Mrs. Dempster was hit on the head by the snowball intended for him, Ramsay has felt a special and intimate relationship to this woman. She appears to him to have worked three miracles: raising his brother Willie from the dead, converting a tramp by an act of Christian charity and appearing to him in the form of a statue of the Madonna when he was near death on the battlefields of Passchendaele. Because of this, Ramsay becomes obsessed with having her officially made a saint. Though she is never canonized, the spiritual force she represents to Ramsay greatly enriches his life. With a deep sense of responsibility, he bears the expense of her care for years until she dies.

Mainly because of his Scottish Presbyterian upbringing, Ramsay has a strong moral conscience. On numerous occasions, most noticeably in his opinions of his friend Boy Staunton, he is highly judgmental of the actions of others. On another occasion, he is critical of the cover-up operation that sentimental people in Weston accomplish in order to preserve the reputation of a lawyer (Orpheus Wettenhall) who has embezzled funds from a number of old people. The only area in which Ramsay is inconsistent in applying his strict moral views concerns money. Although he disapproves of Boy's ruthless business methods, he has no qualms about obtaining financial advice from Boy in order to increase his personal wealth.

Ramsay develops his character most fully through his interaction with Liselotte Vitzlipützli. When he is in his 50s, she points out to him that intelligence and a reverence for the spiritual in life are not enough. Under her influence, Ramsay releases the emotions he has kept under strict control all his life.

Liesl is also the one who points out to Ramsay what particular role he has played during his life. He has been Fifth Business, instrumental in an important way in the lives of others who were more spectacular than himself. On numerous occasions, Ramsay has fulfilled this role. For example, he unwittingly launches Paul's career as a magician by using him as an audience for his magic tricks; he is best man at Boy Staunton's wedding instead of being the bridegroom; he is Boy's confidante; he ghost-writes Eisengrim's autobiography and helps arrange his magic show; he helps Mrs. Dempster behind the scenes; he is, above all, instrumental in the death of Boy Staunton.

Boy Staunton

Boy Staunton, originally named Percy Boyd Staunton and nicknamed "Pidgy Boy-Boy" by his mother, is a wealthy, ambitious industrialist. As a child, he was a "bully, a boast, and certainly a bad loser." At the age of ten, he puts an egg-shaped stone inside the snowball he throws at his friend Dunny Ramsay because he can't stand Dunny having a better sled than his. When the snowball accidentally hits Mary Dempster, it causes her to go into premature labour and makes her simple-minded.

From then on, Boy "edits" his life to avoid taking responsibility for this and other acts that might trouble his conscience. He denies any knowledge of the event when Dunny tries to discuss it with him soon after. Years later, when Boy is in his 60s, he has entirely repressed not only this incident, but any knowledge of the Dempster family as well. But, as Ramsay observes, "He never forgot anything that was of use to him."

Boy is able to "forget" the things that he'd prefer not to think about because of his driving ambitions. He comes from an ambitious family. His father has been one of the two doctors in Deptford. Doc Staunton has become wealthy by investing in real estate around Deptford, especially in large farms that cultivate tobacco and sugar beet crops. He is a selfish man with low moral principles. When there is a serious flu epidemic in Deptford, for example, he "retires" to one of his farms, instead of helping with the numerous patients.

Like his father, Boy has few scruples in his pursuit of wealth and power. He develops the sugar beet investments his father has made into a multi-faceted industry that produces sweet foods under his major corporation called Alpha.

After his expensive education at Colborne College and then in law school in Toronto, Boy marries the prettiest girl in Deptford, Leola Cruikshank. Even during his courtship, however, Boy is unfaithful to her, making frequent visits to Toronto where he met "free-spirited" girls who were not so eager to protect their virtue as Leola. After marriage, since he is preoccupied with sex, he eventually tires of Leola and takes mistresses who cater to his athletic sexuality.

Boy is an exceptionally handsome man. As a college student he drives an expensive, flashy car, and goes around to the dancing places, drinking prohibition liquor from a flask. To Ramsay, he seems like "the quintessence of the Jazz age, a Scott Fitzgerald character." Certainly, he "blossoms in youth," as his name "Boy" suggests. He has glossy, fair hair, dresses expensively and elegantly and moves with style and grace. To many people he looks like a movie star — Richard Barthelmess or Wallace Reid — but the man Boy chose as his model is the glamorous Edward, Prince of Wales. On the Prince's tour of Canada in 1927, Boy manages to secure a position in his entourage as an aide-de-camp. From that time on, Boy uses his "friendship" with the Prince to impress his business acquaintances. He especially prizes the royal silver cup sent to him by the Prince to commemorate the christening of his son, whom he has named Edward David after the Prince.

Ironically, it is the Second World War that brings Boy to the summit of his industrial power, for he is made Minister of Food. This enables him to increase business in his own food industries. For his "war effort" he is awarded the C.B.E. At about the same time, Boy becomes Chairman of the Board at Colborne College, a position that gives him the power to prevent Ramsay from remaining Headmaster of the school after the war.

Boy is chiefly important in the novel as a contrast or foil to Dunstan Ramsay. Whereas Ramsay is interested in spiritual matters, Boy is concerned with material things. Where Ramsay values inner truth, Boy values youth and appearances. Whereas Ramsay wants to let chance play a part in his life, Boy wants to dominate and control everyone and everything. The two men are related to each other by a comparison Ramsay makes to the myth of King Candaules and Gyges. Like this king, Boy wants Ramsay to see his wife naked and asks Ramsay to develop some nude photos of Leola. There are two possible endings to both the modern and the ancient version of this myth. In one, the king loses his wife to his friend (as Boy almost does when Leola tries to seduce Ramsay on Christmas night when Boy walks out). In the other, Gyges kills Candaules (as Ramsay, "the inevitable fifth," partly does to Boy).

Boy's egotism makes him incapable of forming warm human relationships. He neglects Leola once he realizes that his efforts to bring her up to his standards are doomed to failure. He tries to force his son, David, to be manly, not by spending time with him but by taking away his Highlander doll when he is six and by sending him unnecessarily off to boarding school when he is ten. He is especially callous when Leola dies, not even returning from England for her funeral.

Eventually Boy remarries an aggressive, clever divorcée named Denyse Hornick whose ambitions match his own. After failing as a Conservative politician, Boy goes after an appointment as Lieutenant-Governor of Ontario. But as Boy gets older, all the past actions which he has repressed start to come to the surface. Finally, just after he hears that he has been successful in securing the appointment, Ramsay reminds him of the stone-in-the snowball which had caused so much trouble. Boy's resulting guilt is partly responsible for his "suicide."

Paul Dempster

Paul Dempster is prematurely born to the Baptist minister, Amasa Dempster, and his wife, Mary. At first he is a tiny, ugly creature almost covered with "weedy, long black hair." After the first little while in a warm nest of cotton wool devised by Mrs. Ramsay, he impresses her as a "fighter" who will live.

Although Paul does survive his risky infancy, he never looks quite as robust as other children. As a four-year-old, he looked so small and pale that Mrs. Ramsay occasionally wormed him. However, there is nothing wrong with Paul mentally or mechanically. In fact, he proves himself able to accomplish the magic tricks Dunny Ramsay shows him better than the much older Ramsay can do them.

Because his mother is simple enough to have committed adultery with a tramp, Paul's childhood is made miserable by the other children who jeer at him, calling his mother a "hoor." Consequently, Paul feels guilty that his birth has made his mother crazy. So, at the age of nine, shortly after his father dies in the flu epidemic, Paul runs away from home to join a circus. He becomes attached to Willard the Wizard, a conjurer and pick-pocket who teaches him how to conjure in exchange for sexual favours.

Because Willard is a morphine addict who runs into trouble with the police, the circus troupe goes overseas where they call themselves *Le grande Cirque forain de St. Vite*. Paul calls himself Faustus Legrand and does extremely clever card tricks in this show.

The group separates before the Second World War and Paul meets Liesl who renames him Magnus Eisengrim (Eisengrim means "wolf"). Together, they form a magic company and travel to South America. Eisengrim is a wonderfully talented magician whose show emphasizes mystery and wonder rather than cheap comedy. He and Liesl hire Ramsay to ghost-write his autobiography.

When Eisengrim finds out it has not been his fault that his mother became simple, but is really Boy Staunton's fault for putting the stone in the snowball, he apparently doesn't react. However, since Boy's death occurs the same night after Ramsay missed the stone which he used as a paperweight, Eisengrim may have had something to do with his death. Since he is a skilled hypnotist, he may have been "the man who granted his [Boy's] inmost wish."

Mary Dempster

Mary Dempster is the small, pretty woman with "a face like a pan of milk," a soft voice and wavy hair who is the Baptist preacher's wife in Deptford. She is highly unsuited to being a minister's wife for two reasons: she has been used to an easier life with more money where she never learned the practical skills of housekeeping, and her generous nature makes her incapable of living within her husband's small income. Some people think she is a little simple.

She becomes even more simple-minded after she is hit on

the head by a snowball with a stone in it, meant by Percy Boyd Staunton for Dunny Ramsay. The blow and the fall she takes as a result cause her to go into premature labour, and she gives birth to her only child, Paul. Although she is a loving mother, she does not meet Deptford standards of child care. She forgets to cover herself after nursing him and later prefers to keep his hair long and curly rather than short. She and Paul are helped with the tasks necessary for day-to-day existence by the Ramsay family, especially Dunny.

Mrs. Dempster's tendency to give things away combines with her simple-mindedness in an extraordinary act of charity. Meeting a tramp by chance in the gravel pit, she allows him to make love to her. When she is discovered in the act, she says to her husband, "He was very civil, 'Masa. And he wanted it so badly."

After this event, which shocks the townspeople, her husband resigns his job in shame and they move out of the parsonage. He goes to work in the local sawmill and keeps her tied in a harness so she can't get out of the house. Local people make fun of her and her son Paul by calling her a "hoor." The only time she gets out of her harness is when Ramsay comes to get her in an emergency, when his parents have left him with his sick brother Willie. He climbs in the window, as he has often done in secret visits to talk to her and Paul, and cuts her free so that she can assist him. She runs with him to Willie's bedside, where he has apparently stopped breathing, prays and calls him by name. According to Ramsay, she miraculously restores him to life, but the local doctor later disagrees.

To Ramsay, Mrs. Dempster takes on the qualities of a saint, especially after he learns that her adultery with the tramp has converted him into a religious leader. When he is near death in the war, she appears to him in the form of a statue of the Madonna. In this respect, the fact that her name is "Mary" is significant.

Mrs. Dempster becomes distraught at the death of Amasa in the flu epidemic and at the loss of Paul who runs away from home at the age of nine to join the circus. Ramsay finds her staying with her aunt, Miss Bertha Shanklin, at Weston near Toronto. Although she doesn't recognize him, and becomes deeply upset if he talks about Paul, she enjoys his company.

When Miss Shanklin dies, leaving very little money because her lawyer has used her money for his own investments, Ramsay assumes full responsibility for her care. The best he can do for a long time is put her in a public mental institution in Toronto where he can visit her on weekends and holidays. Later, when he can afford to do so, he moves her to a smaller hospital where she can get better care.

Unfortunately, on one of his visits to her, he mentions that he has met her son Paul in Europe and that Paul is helping to pay for her expenses. Mrs. Dempster goes wild at this and attacks Ramsay. Ironically, although it is he who has cared most for her during her life, she considers him her worst enemy for keeping her son from her. In fact, Paul does not want to see his mother because he believes she has been responsible for much of his suffering. From this point on she is kept behind bars and often under sedation. Eventually she dies of a heart attack. Only Ramsay is present at her cremation to mourn her death. He keeps her ashes in a special box.

Leola Cruikshank

Leola Cruikshank, the carpenter's daughter, is the first girl in Deptford for whom Ramsay feels an attraction. She has "cork-screw curls and a great way of never meeting your eyes." Soon, however, Leola is claimed by Percy Boyd Staunton who goes off to Colborne College.

Because Ramsay enlists in the army, and also because Percy does not write very often from school, Leola turns her attention to Ramsay. She promises to love him until he returns from the war.

When Ramsay does return to Deptford after the war, Leola is engaged to Percy. He is relieved because he found her letters to him overseas increasingly dull and boring, but he also resents anyone else having her.

After Leola marries Percy, who by then calls himself "Boy," she discovers that her husband's ambitions include a plan of action for her. At first she rebels against Boy's demands that she acquire such social skills as tennis, bridge and good grammar. As Boy becomes more wealthy and powerful as an industrialist, the ideal he expects Leola to live up to becomes more difficult for her to attain. She chooses pretty, frilly clothes when it is fashionable to wear tailored outfits. She never was able to eliminate what Boy called "hick expressions" like "For Heaven sakes" from her speech. Boy's "idea of a wife for himself would have had the beauty and demeanour of Lady Diana Manners coupled with the wit of Margot Asquith.''

Leola is a weak, stupid woman whose only advantage in life has been her pretty face. She tries to please Boy, but can't. As she becomes middle-aged and after she has two children, "she seemed to relax . . . instead of taking a firmer hold on life.''

Leola's complete devotion to Boy combines with her weak character to make her ineffective in dealing with Boy's domination of her. When he sees she cannot ever be what he wants, Boy neglects her and is unfaithful.

Leola shows her true colours one Christmas when she learns of Boy's unfaithfulness. She demonstrates her weakness by trying to seduce Ramsay. When this is unsuccessful, she attempts to commit suicide by slashing her wrists, but "she was not a good anatomist and had made a gory but not a fatal job of it.'' With the same lack of moral principle with which she became engaged to Boy without first telling Ramsay, she leaves a suicide note blaming Ramsay, not Boy, for her grief.

After this, Leola allows Boy to make all decisions about their children. He removes their son from home to send him to boarding school. Alone and miserable, Leola becomes ill and dies of pneumonia. It is implied that she hastens her own death by opening a window after the nurse has left. Boy, to whom she has remained blindly adoring, does not even come back from England for her funeral.

Diana Marfleet

Diana Marfleet is the beautiful young woman who nurses Ramsay in a private hospital in Buckinghamshire, England. She is a fair-skinned, dark-haired, brown-eyed beauty.

Diana is not a nurse by occupation. In fact, since both her parents are well off, she has no need of an occupation. But like many girls of good background during World War I, she is making her contribution to the war effort by helping look after wounded soldiers.

Diana's father, Canon Marfleet, is a domestic Chaplain to the Royal Family when they visit Windsor Castle, in addition to having a parish of his own. Diana's mother has come from an aristocratic family called De Blaquière. For this reason, Ramsay thinks of her as "Honourable.''

Diana is important in the novel because it is through her that Ramsay makes the final break with his overbearing mother.

Diana falls in love with him and does everything she can to change his dependence on her as a patient into love for her as a husband. But Ramsay eventually realizes that underneath her charm and beauty, Diana is a dominating woman very much like his mother who will always insist on having her own way. It is Diana who "mothers" him in the hospital and teaches him how to use an artificial leg. It is she who corrects his Canadian pronunciation and phrases, initiates him into sexual love and cultural pleasures, and teaches him good manners.

Despite the fact that Ramsay deeply appreciates all that Diana does for him, he "had no intention of being anybody's own dear laddie, ever again." This break from all domineering women, which is really a break from his mother, is symbolized in his renaming. Diana, again like a mother, changes his first name "Dunstable" (his mother's maiden name) into "Dunstan" after St. Dunstan. She then "baptizes" him with some of her father's port. She thus makes him one of the "twice-born," a fact which will have significance later in his life when he meets Liesl.

Liselotte Vitzlipützli

Liesl is a Swiss woman from a family that owns one of the big watch firms. It is her money that sponsors the magic show of Magnus Eisengrim. Liesl is also a brilliant mechanic who assists with the many mechanical devices used in Eisengrim's show. Unlike most mechanics, she is creative because she is able to conceptualize the effect such devices will have when they are completed. This ability enables her to design and construct the elaborate "Brazen Head" that is used for the show.

Liesl is an extraordinarily ugly woman of a generally mannish appearance. She is very tall and strong and she has huge hands and feet. Her hair is cut short and she wears men's clothes. Her jaw is large and juts out, giving her mouth a "monkey-like" appearance. Her eyes are small and deep-set.

Despite her hideous features, however, she is able to seem quite attractive, for her clothes are well-made and of good quality, she moves gracefully and speaks with a beautiful voice in a foreign accent. She is intelligent, cultured and well-educated.

Davies takes the name "Vitzlipützli" from one of the minor devils in Goethe's famous play *Faust*. The name suggests the role Liesl plays in relation to Ramsay, for she tempts him just as the Devil was said to tempt the original St. Dunstan. In that case, the Devil took the form of a fascinating woman, but St. Dunstan was able to resist the temptation by twisting the Devil's nose in his goldsmith's tongs. When Liesl comes to seduce Dunstan Ramsay, he fights her off and finally twists her nose.

But Liesl represents a deeper temptation for Ramsay than that of simple seduction. Since this is a woman of unusual intelligence and intuition, she has great insight into the flaws of Ramsay's character (mainly the fact that he has "buttoned-up" his emotions while he developed his intelligence), and she tempts him to do "something inexplicable, irrational, at the devil's bidding, and just for the hell of it." Her "temptation" ultimately has good results for Ramsay who becomes her lover, her close friend and a wiser man.

Finally, Liesl plays an important role in the plot, for she persuades Eisengrim to allow Ramsay to join the company in order to ghost-write his autobiography. After Boy Staunton's death, it is Liesl, speaking through the "Brazen Head," who answers the question "who killed Boy Staunton?" and thereby causes Ramsay's heart attack.

Themes

Guilt

Davies intended this novel as a study of guilt. In order to demonstrate the complexity of this human emotion, he begins with an event in which it is possible for more than one person to feel guilty. After the snowball with a stone in it hits the pregnant Mary Dempster on the head, causing her great pain, the premature birth of her son, and an apparent decline into simple-mindedness, several people feel guilty.

First of all, Dunny Ramsay, for whom the snowball was intended, feels extremely guilty because he has anticipated that Percy Boyd Staunton with whom he has been quarrelling, will throw one final snowball at him before he goes into his house for dinner. To avoid the snowball he thinks is coming, he dodges around the Dempsters who are out taking a walk. But his guilt is even deeper than this simple situation might suggest. He is just reaching puberty, and eavesdropping on his mother's reports on the premature birth and infancy of Paul Dempster gives him the sickening sense that he is directly involved in "a gross sexual act." His guilt about Mrs. Dempster is thus amplified by the common guilt of adolescence about anything connected with sex. Furthermore, he has been raised in a strict Presbyterian household which has encouraged him to feel guilty about even the smallest lapses from duty.

Second, Paul Dempster himself feels guilty. When he is old enough to understand, he blames himself for causing his mother's simple-mindedness because he has been told that it was his birth that did it. The townspeople worsen his guilt by keeping a distance from him: "the dislike so many people felt for his mother — dislike for the queer and persistently unfortunate — they attached to the unoffending son." After his mother is caught in the act of adultery with a tramp (an act that is blamed on her simple-mindedness), Paul is subjected unfairly to the taunts and jeers of his schoolmates who made rude remarks about his mother.

In contrast to Ramsay and Paul who feel deeply guilty about what has happened to Mrs. Dempster, Percy Boyd Staunton, who not only threw the snowball, but packed an egg-shaped rock into it first, apparently feels no guilt at all. When Ramsay tries to confront him with his responsibility for the event shortly thereafter, Percy says: "I threw a snowball at you and I guess it gave you a good smack." By the time Staunton is 60, he has completely repressed the whole incident even to the point of forgetting who the Dempsters were. When Ramsay reminds him by showing him the stone which he has kept as a paperweight all these years, Boy becomes an angry bully.

Davies demonstrates that guilt, though it is a negative emotion, can ironically produce good results. For example, it is because of his guilt that Ramsay so religiously assumes financial and personal responsibility for Mrs. Dempster. In Boy Staunton's case, however, repressed guilt does considerable damage and ultimately recoils on himself. It is probable that his realization of what he has done, not only directly to Mrs. Dempster but indirectly to Paul, triggers the suicidal wish which is already close to the surface in his mind.

Spirituality versus Materialism

Davies contrasts spiritual values and material values in a central way in this novel. He shows that a life based on material values is shallow and unrewarding while one based on a respect for powers greater than man — no matter how these may be defined — is the only true path to happiness.

Material values in *Fifth Business* are primarily represented by Boy Staunton. Like his father, Boy is more concerned with amassing great wealth and all the possessions money can buy than in spiritual well-being. The only religion Boy is able to understand is the one he becomes enthusiastic about on board ship during his honeymoon. There, the rich Reverend Leadbeater preaches the Christian gospel in a way that reduces everything to economic terms. He sees Christ's miracle at Cana when he turned the water into wine, for example, as Christ "helping the host out of a tight place when the drinks gave out, because He had probably been in the same fix Himself in His days in business." There is nothing more important to Boy than himself and his success. He is an egotist. Therefore, he believes that he can control life by exerting his willpower. He does not clutter his mind with useless information (he never does comprehend what his friend Ramsay is working on and doesn't read his books), but he also never forgets anything that is useful to his advance through life. He values objects (especially if they are expensive). He knows women only as sexual toys, and thinks only in terms of the surface appearance of things. As he gets older, he realizes the sterility of acquiring mere things: "I feel rotten," he tells Ramsay. "I've done just about everything I've ever planned to do, and everybody thinks I'm a success . . . But sometimes I wish I could get into a car and drive away from the whole damned thing."

Spirituality is represented by Dunstan Ramsay. Although he is never destitute, he is not rich enough to be careless with money. But the pursuit of wealth for its own sake does not interest him. He recognizes that there are forces in life beyond his own, and he is happy not to impose his will on life. "I was not sure I wanted to issue orders to life; I rather liked the Greek notion of allowing Chance to take a formative hand in my affairs." Ramsay's scholarly pursuit of information about the saints brings him a deeper joy than anything Boy Staunton has known: "I was . . . a happy goat who had wandered into the wondrous enclosed garden of hagiology, and I grazed greedily and contentedly. When the time came at last for me to go home, I knew I had found a happiness that would endure." Even Ramsay's study of the saints is not the acquisition of knowledge for its own sake. He is also interested in what lies behind the saints. What impulse makes mankind thirst for the miracles that saints perform? As Ramsay gets closer to a comprehension of the reality that lies behind the world of surface appearance, he acquires wisdom and a profound feeling of contentment.

It is worth noting that Ramsay does not find true spiritual values in the people connected with established churches. Amasa Dempster, the Baptist, for example, is too emotional to be charitable to others. Father Regan, the Roman Catholic priest, thinks Mrs. Dempster is only a "fool-saint." All the ministers whom Ramsay meets display more concern for the narrow dogma of the particular sects to which they belong than for the spirit of Christianity. It is only in the eccentric Bollandist, Padre Blazon, who is to a great extent a rebel against the church dogma, that he finds a truly religious spirit.

124

Structure

The novel is structured as a written memoir in six parts. Each part contains several chapters. The titles of the six parts are as follows:
1. Mrs. Dempster
2. I Am Born Again
3. My Fool-Saint
4. Gyges and King Candaules
5. Liesl
6. The Soirée of Illusions

Each of these parts treats a distinct phase of Ramsay's life in chronological order.

Part One: This part is entirely set in Deptford and deals with Ramsay's boyhood from age ten to age 17. Because the story opens with the event that began Ramsay's "lifelong" involvement with Mrs. Dempster, and because it is the section of the book in which she figures most prominently, Part One is named after her.

Part Two: This part begins with Ramsay's participation in the First World War in 1915 and builds up to his return as a veteran and hero to Deptford in 1919. It is called "I Am Born Again" because its high point is the decision Ramsay makes not to marry Diana Marfleet and her renaming of him.

Part Three: This part begins with Ramsay's enrolment at the University of Toronto where he studies history. It ends with his accidental meeting with Paul Dempster in the Tyrol. It is called "My Fool-Saint" because Ramsay's study of the saints leads him to think Mrs. Dempster may be one. He is told, however, that if she is anything, she is a "fool-saint."

Part Four: This part begins with Boy Staunton's financial success in the Depression during the 1930s and concludes with Leola's near-suicide in 1936. It is called "Gyges and King Candaules" because

Ramsay's study of myths leads him to conclude that he and Boy are like modern-day versions of the old legend by that name.

Part Five: This part begins with Boy Staunton's success in the Second World War. It mainly concerns Ramsay's involvement with Magnus Eisengrim's magic show in Mexico. It is called "Liesl" because her temptation of him marks a new stage of development for Ramsay.

Part Six: This part continues Part Five and then moves back to Canada and the bizarre events that surround Boy Staunton's death. It is called "The Soirée of Illusions" because that is the name of Eisengrim's show, and it also refers to an evening in which many illusions are shattered.

Setting

Although Davies spends much more time on character and theme than on setting in *Fifth Business*, the setting is worth noting.

Deptford

Deptford dominates the first section of the novel and also influences the rest. As Ramsay comments, "I left Deptford in the flesh. It was not for a long time that I recognized that I never wholly left it in the spirit." Deptford is important mainly for this reason: its values are the ones that give Ramsay the foundation for his life. It also launches most of the other main characters: Boy Staunton, Leola, Mrs. Dempster and Paul.

Deptford is a small Ontario town that is characterized by its puritanism, its cultural narrowness and its religious hypocrisy. By using satiric description, Davies attacks these shortcomings, but he also shows the good side of small town life. It is, for example, a real community that pulls together when there is an emergency. Many people freely offer assistance to the Ramsay family, for example, when Willie Ramsay needs constant nursing. And when Mrs. Dempster is lost, a volunteer search party is quickly organized. As Ramsay says, "if it had sins and follies and roughnesses, it also had much to show of virtue, dignity, and even of nobility."

Buckinghamshire, England

This is the location of the small private hospital not far from Windsor Castle where Ramsay is nursed back to health after being wounded in the war. It forms a contrast to the battlefield for there is "sweet air — no stink of mud or explosive or corpses or latrines."

It is here that Ramsay first meets Diana Marfleet, the woman he almost marries and who renames him, making him one of the "twice-born."

Toronto

This is where Ramsay attends university and subsequently obtains a job teaching in the private boys' school called Colborne College. He spends most of his adult life in Toronto where one of his friends is Boy Staunton.

Eventually, Boy dies when his car drives into the Toronto

harbour. A solution to the mystery of his death is offered in Eisengrim's magic show which is held at the Royal Alexandra Theatre. Otherwise, few details of Toronto's geography or landmarks are given.

Europe

Ramsay's summer haunt when he does research on the lives of saints. Europe is the scene of wider events, such as the two world wars, and a wealth of history and culture which constitutes a "greater adventure" for Ramsay. It is contrasted with the narrower, more puritanical world of Deptford.

Mexico

Like Europe, Mexico is a setting where the spirit can be enlarged. Ramsay goes to study the shrines there, but is sidetracked into ghost-writing Eisengrim's autobiography.

Style And Technique

Davies' style is a unique blend of several elements. He uses his wide and unusual knowledge to lend an atmosphere of sophistication to all his work. Even the most learned readers will never have heard of some of the myths and books to which Davies refers in his many allusions. Seldom can he refrain from seeing things and describing them in a satiric light. Throughout his writing, he enjoys making fun of the foibles of man in general and Canadians in particular. Because Davies' first love and early training was in drama, he has a good ear for dialogue and the dramatic qualities in a scene of action. His descriptive passages are characterized by an unusual liveliness that arises from the fresh or colourful words and phrases he uses. To many readers, Davies' style is the most enjoyable aspect of his work.

Allusion

An allusion is a reference to something (most often another literary work) that lies outside the sphere of the text itself. *Fifth Business* is a novel full of allusions used in a variety of ways. For example, Davies makes an allusion to the myth of Gyges and King Candaules as the title and frame of reference for Part Four of the book. He draws a comparison between Gyges and Ramsay, and between King Candaules and Boy Staunton to show that people still behave as they did centuries ago. On another occasion, Davies uses allusion for comic effect when he names the three women Ramsay goes out with while he is teaching at Colborne College: Agnes Day, Gloria Mundy and Libby Doe. The first two names are allusions to the Latin phrases from the church service: *agnus dei* (lamb of God) and *gloria mundi* (the glory of the world). The third is an allusion to the sexual and pleasure-loving aspect of human personality in Freud's psychology: *libido*. Since each of these women have personalities that match the allusion, it can be seen as an effective comic technique, a joke between Davies and the reader.

Satire

Satire is the use of ridicule or irony to expose the follies and vices of man. Davies uses both methods — ridicule and irony — to attack the actions and attitudes he dislikes. In describing the concert that marked his return as a hero to Deptford, Ramsay says, "Muriel Parkinson sang about the Rose that Blows in

129

No-Man's Land, and when she shrieked (for her voice was powerful rather than sweet) that 'mid'st the war's great curse stood the Red Cross Nurse,' many people mopped their eyes." A good example of the ironical form of satire occurs when Ramsay shows himself and Boy discussing the dreadful hardship of the Depression. When Boy says, "at present I feel I should do everything I can to see that people have necessities," Ramsay immediately observes: "And we both took reflective pulls at the excellent whiskies-and-soda he had provided." Since Ramsay, the narrator himself, is noted as a boy for "getting off 'good ones' " and in old age is "a sharp-tongued old man," this satire can be seen as an aspect of his characterization.

Dialogue and Dramatic Qualities

Almost any scene in this novel can be analyzed from a dramatic point of view, though some scenes are more striking than others. The scene in which Mrs. Dempster is apprehended with the tramp, Ramsay's last hours on the battlefield at Passchendaele, and his fight with Liesl, for example, all have the quick pace and good timing that audiences expect in the best plays. Davies has a good ear for dialogue. He gives Milo Papple, the town's barber, the bad grammar and slang expressions that he would undoubtedly use. To Mrs. Ramsay, he gives expressions that are suited to her, such as Mrs. Dempster had "a face like a pan of milk." To Ramsay, he gives a satiric turn of expression that is entirely in character. With a sense of the book's overall impact, Davies is careful to put side by side scenes that contrast with one another. Thus, a comic scene is often put next to a more serious one and a scene about Boy is placed next to a scene about Ramsay.

Language

Davies' language is highly coloured and unusually fresh. Ramsay notes, for example, that King George has "very blue, rather glittering eyes," when he receives his V.C. Leola is described on one occasion as "all curls and soft whispers." The infamous lawyer, Orpheus Wettenhall, is "a gallant little particle." The scenery onstage when Ramsay attends his homecoming concert in Deptford is "toxic." Davies draws on his extremely wide vocabulary to find the accurate term for what he describes. A church in Mexico is a "basilica"; one who studies the saints is a "hagiographer"; a conjurer does tricks by "sleight of hand" and is called a "*prestidigitateur*." The use of such precise terms, often drawn from languages other than English, gives Davies' prose a sophisticated and substantial air. Davies avoids clichés (common expressions) except for characterization in dialogue or when he wishes to make fun of the cliché. For example, he has Ramsay say that his mother "with her unfailing good sense, hit the nail on the head." Although "hit the nail on the head" is a cliché, Davies deliberately uses it tongue-in-cheek here to show that his mother was an aggressive overbearing sort of woman.

Point of View

Davies employs the first person point of view in *Fifth Business*. Ramsay tells us his own story throughout. In this respect, the novel is like Bronte's *Jane Eyre* or Dickens' *David Copperfield*. This point of view is much more likely to involve the reader than the third person or omniscient point of view because events are told firsthand, complete with all the emotional impact they had at the time.

The main problem with first person narration is its relativity. Events are told only as they seem to the narrator, and the reader has no way of measuring the accuracy of his account. For the author, first person poses problems of plot development because he can only legitimately include events and conversations that his narrator has actually participated in. Usually, as in *Fifth Business*, a good deal of information must be conveyed by means of stories told to the narrator which he then relates to someone else. In *Fifth Business*, this is accomplished by having Ramsay write his memoirs to his Headmaster. At the point at which he recalls incidents that the Headmaster would already know about, Davies somewhat awkwardly has Ramsay tell him that he is going to "refresh his memory."

On the whole, *Fifth Business* is an example of first person narration done well. Davies helps the reader feel confidence in his single storyteller by making Ramsay an extremely precise and careful observer and by having him a trained historian. Because Ramsay is writing in anger to tell the Headmaster what his life has actually been like, there is plenty of emotion and drama to interest the reader. In addition, Davies uses mysterious circumstances, such as Boy Staunton's death, and the various reappearances of Paul Dempster, to keep the reader in suspense.

Selected Criticisms

The rich incidents and characterizations are reminiscent of 19th-Century fiction, but will appeal to modern tastes.
Ruth Nadelhaft, *Christian Science Monitor* (Dec. 31, 1970)

Davies' novel is intelligently conceived and intelligently narrated, free from gimmicks and tricks; not at all mod, it makes no appeals to current fashions in style or content, neither pandering to the reader nor taking on the universe, but is full of the art that conceals itself . . . Ramsay is a pleasure because he is so intelligent — not bookish and allusive, but perceptive. He knows a lot about life, including his own, and says what he knows briefly and well, not in [a] pontifical manner . . . but tersely, quietly, and unostentatiously.
J.D. O'Hara, *Newsweek* (Jan. 18, 1971)

[This] is a mature, accomplished and altogether remarkable book, one of the best of this or any other season, and it simply cannot be ignored . . . [it] achieves a richness and depth that are exceptional in a modern novel . . . Davies writes in a clear and deceptively simple style.
Sister M.W. Brady, *Best Sell* (Feb. 1, 1971)

The notion of Fifth Business is effective in providing a central image for Ramsay's character. The fall from the heroic which it implies is familiar in modern literature. "I am not Hamlet, nor was meant to be," J. Alfred Prufrock confides in us, sensing that he is a kind of Fifth Business. And Tom Stoppard's *Rosencrantz and Guildenstern Are Dead* shifts the point of view on *Hamlet* in order that the futility of heroism be shown. Dunstan Ramsay, though, on occasion seems far from "inglorious." The traditional heroism which wins him the V.C., for instance, or his academic success despite difficult circumstances, or the later publication of his books — all these are more "heroic" than the concept of Fifth Business implies.
Elspeth Buitenhuis (Cameron), *Robertson Davies* (Forum House, 1972)

Dunstan orders his story, it seems, to dramatize how two interlocking constellations of characters play their parts in his unfolding physical and spiritual life. One constellation asserts forces primarily on his outer, public life, and at the end of the story enables him to recognize himself as "Fifth Business," his shadow side. This constellation includes Boyd (Boy) Staunton, Boy's first and second wives, Leola and Denyse, and Paul Dempster, son of Mrs. Mary Dempster. The other constellation dramatizes his inner search for his image: his mother, Mrs. Mary Dempster, Leola, Diana Marfleet, and finally, Liesl. Two priests, one in his village and one in his private life, add their direction: Father Regan dogmatically warns him against pursuing a "fool-saint;" Father Blazon acts as his Wise Old Man, and directs the pursuit of the spirit inward. Mary Dempster in her changing aspects is the major interlocking force between the two constellations.

Gordon Roper, *Journal of Canadian Fiction* (Winter, 1972)

[Davies'] talent has blossomed into a rare genius. *Fifth Business* is one of the most accomplished and mature novels to have been published in recent years and, while the protagonist, Dunstable Ramsay, is in a form of exile in his lifelong search for the meaning of sainthood and of himself, there is nothing whatsoever that is colonial about his quest.

John Moss, *Patterns of Isolation*
(McClelland & Stewart, 1974)

Fifth Business is the master work of the Deptford trilogy . . . Only in *Fifth Business* does Davies create an organic whole from his disparate materials. All information is connected to the book's central character, reflecting his interests, showing us how he thinks, influencing his life, and playing a part in his interpretation of events.

Judith Grant, *Robertson Davies*
(McClelland & Stewart, 1978)

Davies' characters have too sparse an identity beyond their obsessive quirks and allusions. And a novel, covering 60 years in the form of a 300-page letter, suffers for want of dramatic tension.

Martin Levin, *Library Journal* (Nov. 1, 1979)

Suggested Study Topics

1. Davies has explained that he originally planned *Fifth Business* to be about guilt: "Where did it arise? At what age was a human creature capable of feeling and assuming the burden of guilt? Were the truly guilty always as burdened as were those whose upbringing and moral training disposed them to feel guilt and perhaps also to assume guilt which was not truly theirs?" How are these questions presented and answered in the novel?

2. What are the advantages and disadvantages of using the first person point of view? How does Davies try to counteract the disadvantages of this method of narration? Is he successful?

3. What does "Fifth Business" mean? How does Davies use the idea in developing the character of Dunstan Ramsay?

4. What aspects of the relationship of illusion and reality does Davies explore in this novel? What does he see as the function of illusion in modern life?

5. As a social document, what does *Fifth Business* demonstrate about the nature of small town life in the first half of the 20th century?

6. There are many ministers in this novel. List them, write a brief character sketch for each and use this information to develop an essay on religion in *Fifth Business*.

7. Davies is sometimes accused of relying too heavily on coincidence to advance his plots. In your opinion, is this true of *Fifth Business*? List all the coincidences you find in the novel and discuss whether or not they are probable or improbable.

8. Davies began his career not as a novelist but as a dramatist. Discuss the influence his training in drama has had on this novel.

9. It has been said that the satirist is a person with a grievance. Examine Davies' satiric description of Ramsay's return to Deptford as a hero after the war in Part Two, Chapter 7. What grievances does Davies have about this celebration? What techniques does he use as a satirist?

10. When he was asked what he was trying to do when he wrote *Fifth Business*, Davies replied that he was "trying to record the bizarre and passionate life of Canadian people." Do you think he succeeds in doing this?

11. Why is *Fifth Business* divided into six parts? What is the significance of the titles of these parts?

12. Define the following, and briefly state (in one or two sentences) the significance of each:
    a) hagiographer
    b) polymath
    c) geek
    d) fool-saint
    e) Bollandist
    f) atheist
    g) ghost-write

13. In what ways is Boy Staunton used as a "foil" to help characterize Dunstan Ramsay?

14. Davies has written elsewhere that the concept of the "unlived life" needs fuller explanation: "It is not suggested that we should all obey every prompting of our desires, though it is healthy for us to give full attention to those desires which will not fulfill, but which sometimes arise to plague us. We must be aware of the darker side of our natures." Discuss this idea in relation to Ramsay's encounter with Liesl and the events that lead up to it. Are there other characters in the novel to whom the same theory might apply?

15. Which opening chapter of those that begin the six parts of the novel is most effective? Why?

Bibliography

Baltensperger, Peter. "Battles with the Trolls," *Canadian Literature*, No. 71 (Winter 1976), pp. 59-67.

Bjerring, Nancy E. "Deep in the Old Man's Puzzle," *Canadian Literature*, No. 62 (Autumn 1974), pp. 49-60.

Brown, R. and D. Bennett. "Magnus Eisengrim: The Shadow of the Trickster in the Novels of Robertson Davies," *Modern Fiction Studies*, No. 22 (1976), pp. 347-63.

Buitenhuis (Cameron), Elspeth. *Robertson Davies*. Toronto: Forum House, 1972.

Callwood, June. "The Beard," *Maclean's Magazine*, 15 March 1972, pp. 16-17, 30-33.

Cameron, Donald. "Robertson Davies: The Bizarre and Passionate Life of the Canadian People," *Conversations with Canadian Novelists, Part One*. Toronto: Macmillan of Canada, 1973, pp. 30-48.

Cude, Wilfred. "Miracle and Art in *Fifth Business*; or, Who the Devil is Liselotte Vitzlipützli?" *Journal of Canadian Studies*, No. 9, no. 4 (1974), pp. 3-16.

de Villiers, Marq. "The Master's World," *The Globe and Mail Weekend Magazine*, 15 Nov. 1975, pp. 8-10, 12.

Gerson, Carole. "Dunstan Ramsay's Personal Mythology," *Essays on Canadian Writing*, No. 6 (Spring 1977), pp. 100-108.

Grant, Judith. *Robertson Davies*. Toronto: McClelland & Stewart, 1978.

Harpur, Tom. "Author Says Messiah Could Be A Woman," *Toronto Daily Star*, 16 Feb. 1974, p. F5.

Hetherington, Renée and Gabriel Kampf. "*Acta* Interviews *Robertson Davies*," *Acta Victoriana*, No. 97, no. 2 (1973), pp. 69-87.

Lawrence, Robert and Samuel Macy, eds. *Studies in Robertson Davies' Deptford Trilogy*, No. 20, ELS Monograph Series, University of Victoria, 1980.

McPherson, Hugo. "The Mask of Satire: Character and Symbolic Pattern in Robertson Davies' Fiction," *Canadian Literature*, No. 4 (Spring 1960), pp. 18-30.

Monaghan, David M. "Metaphors and Confusions," *Canadian Literature*, No. 67 (Winter 1976), pp. 64-73.

Monk, Patricia. "Confessions of a Sorcerer's Apprentice: *World of Wonders* and the Deptford Trilogy of Robertson Davies," *Dalhousie Review*, No. 56 (Summer 1976), pp. 366-72.

_____. "Psychology and Myth in *The Manticore*," *Studies in Canadian Literature*, No. 2 (1977), pp. 69-81.

Morley, Patricia. *Robertson Davies*. Profiles in Canadian Drama Series. Toronto: Gage Educational Publishing, 1977.

Moss, John. *Patterns of Isolation*. Toronto: McClelland & Stewart, 1974.

Neufeld, James. "Structural Unity in 'The Deptford Trilogy': Robertson Davies as Egoist," *Journal of Canadian Studies*, No. 12, no. 1 (1977), pp. 68-74.

Owen, Ivon. "The Salterton Novels," *Tamarack Review*, No. 9 (Autumn 1958), pp. 56-63.

Roper, Gordon. "A Davies Log," *Journal of Canadian Studies*, No. 12, no. 1 (1977), pp. 4-19.

_____. "Robertson Davies' *Fifth Business* and 'That Old Fantastical Duke of Dark Corners, C.G. Jung'." *Journal of Canadian Fiction*, No. 1, no. 1 (Winter 1972), pp. 33-9.

Steinberg, M.W. "Don Quixote and the Puppets: Theme and Structure in Robertson Davies' Drama," *Canadian Literature*, No. 7 (Winter 1961), pp. 45-53.